Easykayaking Basics

A Paddling Handbook for the Pacific Northwest

Easykayaking Basics

A Paddling Handbook for the Pacific Northwest

Gary Backlund and Paul Grey

Harbour Publishing

The writers, editors and publishers of *Easykayaking Basics: A Paddling Handbook for the Pacific Northwest* have made every effort to ensure the reader's awareness of accessibility, hazards and level of expertise involved in the activities described, but your own safety is ultimately up to you. We take no responsibility for any loss or injury incurred by anyone using this book. If you spot any inaccuracies let us know.

Published by Harbour Publishing Co. Ltd., P.O. Box 219, Madeira Park, BC V0N 2H0
www.harbourpublishing.com

Cover design by Martin Nichols • Page design by Roger Handling
Cover photo by Keith Thirkell • Illustrations by Janice Blaine except where otherwise noted
Photos by Gary Backlund and Paul Grey except where otherwise noted.

Photographs courtesy of Mountain Equipment Co-op on pages 30, 31, 32, 33, 49, 50, 53, 55, 57, 70, 75, 76, 77, 81, 82, 83, 84, 85, 86, 88, 90, 123, 127, 134, 138; courtesy of Current Designs 1, 22, 39, 40, 46, 48, 50, 51, 55, 73, 78, 113, 132; courtesy of Seaward Kayaks 2, 5, 10, 14, 18, 27, 28, 43, 44, 58, 94, 96, 115, 122, 125, 130, 143, 145, 146, 151; photographs by Katherine Backlund, 9, 59, 141; by Teesh Backlund, 12, 20, 34, 36, 100, 107, 111; by Gary Doran, 6; by Brian Henry, 135; by Greg Shea, 112; by Jacqueline Windh, 19.
Illustrations courtesy of Yakima on pages 60, 62, 63, 64.

Printed and bound in Canada

Harbour Publishing acknowledges financial support from the Government of Canada through the Book Publishing Industry Development Program and the Canada Council for the Arts, and from the Province of British Columbia through the British Columbia Arts Council and the Book Publisher's Tax Credit through the Ministry of Provincial Revenue.

THE CANADA COUNCIL | LE CONSEIL DES ARTS
FOR THE ARTS | DU CANADA
SINCE 1957 | DEPUIS 1957

BRITISH
COLUMBIA
ARTS COUNCIL
Supported by the Province of British Columbia

National Library of Canada Cataloguing in Publication

Backlund, Gary, 1951-
    Easykayaking basics : a paddling handbook for the Pacific Northwest / Gary Backlund, Paul Grey. — 1st ed.

Includes index.
ISBN 1-55017-309-X

    1. Kayaking—Northwest, Pacific—Guidebooks. I. Grey, Paul, 1951- II. Title.

GV783.B33 2004   797.1'224'09711   C2004-900643-6

Contents

Acknowledgements

The authors of *Easykayaking Basics: A Paddling Handbook for the Pacific Northwest* are greatly indebted to the following people and groups who shared their time and knowledge in order to make your future paddling safer and more enjoyable. Our thanks to you all.

Life is a learning experience; our time with groups such as the Nanaimo Paddlers Club certainly reinforces this.

The following equipment manufacturers were extremely knowledgeable and took the time to give us tours and answer our seemingly endless questions: Brooks, Whites Manufacturing, Danforth and Aquameter Compasses, Bill Emile of Scotty, Dave Bain of Nimbus Paddles, Protexion Products (Buoy-O-Boy PFDs), Ian Race and the people of Current Designs for a great tour of their factory, Seaward Kayaks, Steve Wagner of Salus Marine Wear, Ross Wyborn of Serratus and Colin Bixby of All Seasons Auto-Racks.

Island Outdoor Centre in Ladysmith and Alberni Outpost in Nanaimo allowed us to disrupt business in order to photograph equipment, boats and displays. These two retailers are great places to learn more about equipment, as are most paddling stores.

Lynda Evans of Ladysmith Physiotherapy Clinic helped with paddling warm-upss and exercises.

A number of other groups made essential contributions, including the Canadian Coast Guard, the Labatt WaterWise Boat Safety Team and the Office of Boating Safety (in particular Jean Pontbriand, for information regarding PFDs).

Special thanks goes to our families, who saw us through the trials and tribulations of producing our third kayaking book. We give a very big thank you to Teesh Backlund for her many hours of editing and proofreading, and for her suggested improvements.

The staff and editors at Harbour Publishing have gently led us through a maze of procedures and helped us navigate the realms of publishing. They've done a great job of guiding, editing and marketing. We can't say enough about their patience and hard work.

And finally, thanks to all the friendly folk we met and visited while researching and paddling our way through this book. It was your questions and comments that helped shape it.

Welcome to Easykayaking Basics

Learning to kayak the hard way, by trial and error, isn't much fun and can be costly or even dangerous. This book provides beginning and intermediate kayakers with useful information to make their journey easier and safer. In *Easykayaking Basics: A Paddling Handbook for the Pacific Northwest*, we've included many web sites and other sources for additional information. These are also available through links at our site: www.easykayaker.com.

The seemingly simple task of buying the right kayaking equipment and clothing isn't all that simple. Even choosing an appropriate paddle is more difficult than it sounds. Given the cost of a paddle, you don't want to be purchasing several before finding the right one. The big-ticket item, though, is a new or used kayak. We speak from experience, having acquired and sold many kayaks, paddles and other pieces of equipment in what seems like a continual upgrading process. If we had known then what we know now... With all these concerns in mind, we've written this book to pass on some words of wisdom. We hope our experiences will enable you to make educated choices when navigating the twisted waters of kayak equipment consumerism. All prices given are in Canadian dollars.

Once you've decided to head off paddling for a fun day or week, we want to help you have a really enjoyable time on the water, not a kayaking trip from hell or just a ho-hum experience. To do this, we pass on information about harnessing the tides and the wind, knowing when to stay safely on shore, understanding the particulars of marine camping and avoiding some of the more common pitfalls of sea kayaking.

What is obvious to many of us salty Westcoasters may not be so evident to beginners or to folk who come to the Pacific Northwest from other parts of Canada or the world. In this book, we provide common sense and a whole lot of advice on how to make your paddling time and trips more enjoyable.

Remember Goldilocks and the three bears? Things were too hot, too cold, too hard, too soft, too big and too little. When we go paddling, we don't want cold wet feet in the winter, nor do we want to feel as if our feet are mired in a hot bowl of porridge in midsummer. We don't want to be cold because we have the wrong paddling top, nor do we want to cook under a drytop when the sun pops out.

Easykayaking Basics

Comfort is important as we sit hour after hour gently paddling the beautiful Pacific coastline. In a kayak, a well-designed padded seat and proper-fitting thigh braces are necessary to provide a high level of comfort. It's also important to have a kayak and paddle that make paddling a joy and allow you to keep up with others without working too hard. It seems Goldie really wasn't too much different from us. And, yes, we occasionally see the three bears when out paddling, so we offer some safety advice for when you're travelling in bear country.

Gary and Paul at Evening Cove

Kayaking is considered "soft adventure" and has some inherent risks, such as staying upright during adverse conditions. In a sense, it's the equivalent of riding a bicycle, only you're on water. When you stop and think about it, though, kayaks are only about 60 cm (2 ft) wide, and you're taking on the Pacific Ocean. There's an element of danger involved. From what we've seen and heard, it's surprising that so few people get into serious trouble. That's what a big part of this book is about: safety.

If you want to get the most out of your paddling adventures, this book is written for you. Once your PFD is zipped and buckled, and you've eased your legs and backside into the cockpit and briefly struggled to stretch the sprayskirt over the coaming, you're finally off to paddle the briny blue. For some reason everyone is humming the theme song from Gilligan's Island. Gilligan and crew had fun (who wouldn't with Mary Ann along), and that is this book's ultimate purpose: to make kayaking an enjoyable experience.

Gary Backlund & Paul Grey

Section 1
Getting Ready

1 Buying a sea kayak

If you haven't done much paddling, buying your first kayak can be a difficult decision-making process. As the saying goes, good judgment comes from experience and experience comes from bad judgment. Reading about kayak design and talking to experienced kayakers will help. Talking to fanatical kayakers may just confuse you, however, as boat design and performance is a never-ending topic with these people. Just as beauty is in the eye of the beholder, kayaks appeal to different people in different ways. One size doesn't fit all and levels of experience, stability, comfort, intended use and other factors must also be weighed.

Finding a kayak that fits makes for comfortable paddling.

There are several ways to get to know a model before you part with your cash. Going for a test paddle is a must, and not just a five-minute, calm-water experience. Renting or borrowing a variety of kayaks and trying them out is the best preparation you can make before purchasing your own. (See Test Paddling, page 21.)

When choosing a kayak, you need to decide if you want a single or a double and how important stability is to you. Buying new allows you to choose the colour and options. Buying used saves money.

KNOWING WHAT YOU'RE LOOKING FOR

Type and style considerations

- single or double
- stability and/or speed
- carrying capacity for longer trips (storage volume)
- soft or hard chine
- degree of rocker
- symmetrical, fish or swedeform
- bow design
- rudder, skeg

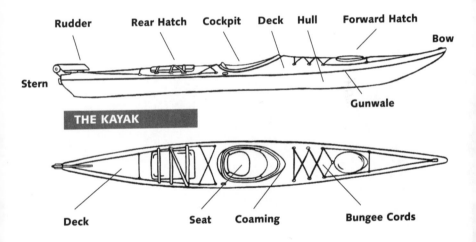

THE KAYAK

Preliminary decisions and terminology:

Before choosing and purchasing a kayak, there are several decisions you'll have to make.

Single (K1) or double (K2)

Do you want a single or a double kayak? Doubles are very stable but not nearly as much fun to paddle as singles. Eventually, most kayakers prefer a single. Doubles are more difficult to return to an upright position and pump out, if you capsize. Double kayaks are heavy; it may require four people to carry a fully loaded double from the water up the beach. Even if your intent is mainly day paddling, lifting a double on and off a vehicle can be quite a challenge, especially for weaker people.

Day paddler or expedition kayaker?

What type of paddling are you planning to do: day trips, overnighters or week-long journeys? What kind of paddler do you want to be: fair-weather or all-weather? The answers to these questions will dictate the size of the kayak that will best fit your needs. Keep in mind that your plans may expand as you get into the sport.

Volume

Kayak specifications usually show the total volume of the boat and the volume of each cargo hold. The larger the overall volume, the more weight the boat will carry. Larger cargo areas can hold more camping supplies. Paddling a large empty boat can mean extra work

Gary testing a Seaward Vision.

Buying

on windy days, as wind resistance and waves slapping against your kayak will both have an impact on your travel speed. For some paddlers, larger may mean that the boat will handle a bit like a tank. Many larger kayak models come in either a standard size or a high-volume version, which is usually about 18 mm (0.75 in) deeper where the hull and deck join. The extra depth of a high-volume boat also creates more legroom for getting in and out of the cockpit.

Cockpit size

There are three standard cockpit-opening sizes, depending on the model of the kayak. Smaller sizes can be difficult for tall people, heavier people and people who don't bend well.

Speed

Generally, the longer and narrower the kayak, the faster it is. Calling a boat "fast" seems out of place when talking about recreational paddling, as speed is not the main issue. A faster boat, however, slides through the water gracefully, with little effort, and is a real joy to paddle. As a result, the distance that a person can cover increases, new paddling areas become accessible and it's less work to keep up with the rest of your group.

Stability

Stability, on the other hand, is essential to safety. Slipping through the water with ease is only great if you can do it right side up. Most popular ocean-touring single kayaks are between 55 and 62 cm (22 and 25 in) wide.

There are two aspects of stability. Initial stability is how tippy a kayak feels when you are sitting still in calm water. If the boat shifts dramatically every time you move, photography, fishing and other activities can be awkward and it's hard to relax. Secondary stability refers to how prone the boat is to capsizing. Good primary stability, for instance, allows a boat to feel very stable as you enjoy a cup of hot tea from your thermos; good secondary stability means you can lean over the side and pull up your crab trap without joining the crabs in the water. Most rental outfits and adventure tour guides buy kayaks that have both good initial and secondary stability. Some kayaks have one but not the other. The best way to test stability is by getting wet. It may involve a pool session in the winter or a refreshing ocean or lake swim in summer.

Soft or hard chine

The chine (transition between the sides and the bottom of the hull) and the shape of the bottom contribute significantly toward stability. Normally, a soft chine (rounded transition) and a flat but somewhat rounded bottom give the best stability. A hard chine sacrifices initial stability for speed and playfulness.

Hull shapes and tracking

Hull shapes may be symmetrical, fish form or swedeform. Fish form means that the widest part of the boat is forward of centre; swedeform means the widest part is aft; symmetrical boats are the same width forward and aft. Hull shapes and rocker (upward curva-

HULL SHAPES

Symmetrical

Fish Form

Swedeform

Soft Chine   **Hard Chine**

Rounded Bottom   **Flat Bottom**

ture of the keel) affect tracking and turning, as well as speed and stability. A boat with little rocker goes straight, even when you don't want it to, whereas a boat with too much rocker will turn on a dime and can be a challenge to steer when paddling with a tailwind. Too much rocker can also detract from secondary stability.

You should also consider flare (the shape of the sides) and whether you want a swept-up bow (Greenland style) or more of a straight nose to your boat. A swept-up bow catches the wind and can get slapped by waves, yet may surf better. Many kayakers think it looks better, too.

Rudder or skeg

Does the boat have a rudder or skeg (a retractable or fixed fin located on the keel near the stern to improve tracking)? Will you need one? Although you may paddle for weeks on end without ever needing a rudder or skeg, if you encounter high winds, or even mild currents, you'll be thankful for one. A rudder, unlike a skeg, swivels and helps you turn. Foot controls for rudders vary greatly, as do methods for raising and lowering the rudder blade. Some systems are easier to operate than others.

Rotomoulded kayaks are less expensive but have shorter lifespans.

Colour

Dark colours show scratches more. This is why most kayak bottoms are white. Yellow hulls, which are easier to spot than white hulls when upside down in whitecaps, may be harder to spot washed up on a beach. Unfortunately, if you plan to use your kayak in California or Mexico, yellow seems to attract great white sharks. Bright deck colours make your kayak more visible to larger boats and, therefore, are safer. Some manufacturers offer a wide variety of colours and patterns, including faded, metallic and splatter designs, though these are difficult to touch up.

Materials
COMPOSITE

Composite (fibreglass and Kevlar) kayaks are beautiful, with graceful lines and rich colours. Made in two pieces (hull and deck)

You can paddle all day in the right kayak.

and then joined with a seam, they consist of an outer surface of gel coat over layers of fibreglass or Kevlar mat mopped with resin. Kevlar, which is strong but difficult to repair, reduces the kayak's weight by about 2.5 kg (5.5 lb). Many women and older paddlers are now purchasing Kevlar models for the weight advantage, though they are more expensive. The lighter material doesn't really affect paddling.

ADVANTAGES
- more attractive than kayaks constructed from most other materials
- faster in the water than most plastic, wood and skin kayaks because of the gel coat finish
- easily repairable (except Kevlar)
- can be waxed for better speed
- can last up to 30 years, if protected from ultraviolet (UV) rays
- lighter weight than plastic kayaks
- good resale value

Buying

DISADVANTAGES
- expensive
- scratch easily
- heavier than wood or skin

ROTOMOULDED

Rotomoulded (polyethylene—aka plastic) kayaks are heat-formed as a single piece; hence, they are only one colour. They are often chosen as starter boats before moving up to a composite kayak.

ADVANTAGES
- significantly less expensive than composite kayaks
- much stronger than composite, more damage-proof

DISADVANTAGES
- slower in the water than a composite
- difficult to repair
- heavier than composite, wood or skin
- lifespans as short as eight years, if exposed to UV rays for prolonged periods
- don't hold resale value as well as composite

WOOD

Wood kayaks are often beautiful, owner-built pieces of art. They are normally quite light. If you are at the point of constructing a wood craft, you have likely studied design, handling and other characteristics, and have made a personal choice for wood.

There are two distinctly different methods of wood-kayak construction. One is "stitch and sew," where pieces of thin marine plywood are sewn together using thin wire. The seams are then sealed with fibreglass strips and resin. The other method is "strip" construction, where the kayak is made from many thin strips of wood (such as

Lovingly hand built, wood kayaks are often works of art.

cedar). Both types are then coated with fibreglass resin or epoxy. "Stitch and sew" kayaks are usually hard chine, due to the nature of their construction, while "strip" boats can be either soft or hard chine. The methods also differ greatly in terms of the number of hours involved. A "stitch and sew" kayak is relatively quick and easy to build compared to a "strip" boat.

ADVANTAGES
• usually less expensive than composite, especially if you build it yourself
• the beauty and warm appeal of wood
• the satisfaction of building your own kayak
• often a work of art
• lighter than most other types
• kits and courses are commercially available

DISADVANTAGES
• may require a little more pampering and care than composite and rotomoulded kayaks
• not quite as strong as composite and rotomoulded
• may not be as comfortable as factory-made
• may not have a high resale value
• can be a problem to buy used, especially if handmade, as it's hard to tell if it's well-built or not

Skin kayaks are very lightweight and have a traditional look.

Buying

SKIN

Skin kayaks are made by stretching and sewing a layer of nylon, polyester or canvas over a lightweight wooden or aluminum frame. The skin is sealed and hardened with urethane or another type of finish. Surprisingly, the skin is quite tough. These boats look unique and are made more in the tradition of ancient kayaks.

ADVANTAGES
- usually less expensive than composite, especially if you build it yourself
- the satisfaction of building your own kayak
- often a work of art (at least, to the owner)
- lighter than most other types of kayaks
- kits and classes are commercially available

DISADVANTAGES
- slower than other types (depending on smoothness of exterior finish)
- may not be as comfortable as factory-made
- requires more pampering and care
- not as strong
- may not have a high resale value
- can be a problem to buy used, especially if handmade, as it's hard to tell if well-built

Test paddling

Always do at least a two-hour test paddle before buying. Although you can test many models at various paddlefests and kayak demo-days, it is best to either rent or take a guided trip with a particular make or model.

A good way to judge a kayak is to take a day-long paddle in various water conditions. Many wise consumers now book outfitter-guided trips that guarantee the models of boats they will be paddling. Make sure you take some padding along, to see if you can achieve a comfortable fit. A day in an ill-fitting cockpit can be agony. Sometimes a better fit can be achieved with a little cushioning.

Test how the boat handles when empty and loaded. If you plan to use the kayak for mostly overnight trips, load the hatches full with gear, not rocks. Loading with rocks or water bottles will give a very low centre of gravity and more stability than normal.

Double kayaks offer greater stability.

If you are limited to a short paddle, try to do it on a windy day with somewhat rough water conditions. See how the boat tracks both upwind and downwind. If possible, find some boat traffic and see how the kayak takes large waves (wakes) from different angles. If it's warm enough for a swim, find out how well the boat edges (see Edging and Leaning, page 110) and at what point it tips over. Try a power paddle; by paddling hard, you'll be able to see if the hull slips gracefully through the ocean or if it pushes water.

Other things to test are the rudder controls, ease of opening and closing hatches, and bungee layout for holding your water bottle, chart, pump, throw bag, paddle float and spare paddle. Cockpit-rim size and thigh bracing should be checked for fit; you should be able to get in the kayak easily, but once in, you should feel like you are wearing the boat.

Lastly, try several different makes and models. You'll learn a little more with each one. Make notes on what you like and don't like, as features can be hard to remember after trying out five or more models. If you are undecided whether to buy fibreglass or plastic, rent two similar kayaks, one of each type, and go for a paddle with a friend. Change boats mid-trip—it might be quite an eye opener.

You can contact manufacturers to find out the closest dealers or

rental locations for their models. Manufacturers will often refund any rental costs if you purchase a boat from them. Some manufacturers and dealers keep small fleets for this purpose.

Bottom line

If you aren't an expert in kayak design (and even the experts disagree), it's time to rely on some basic principles. Does the boat feel good when you paddle normally? How does it feel when you try a power paddle at full speed? A short power paddle is a good way to tell how the boat will handle under rougher weather conditions and how well it slips through the water. Is this a model that outfitters and rental companies buy? Do you like the look of the kayak? Does it fit you well? The seat should feel comfortable and give good back support.

Once the single-vs-double question has been decided, most people compromise. They look for a boat that is great for day paddles and yet suitable for extended trips. Stability usually wins out over speed. If gale force winds catch you out on the water, having an extra 5 cm (2 in) in width will certainly increase your comfort level.

Our experience (Gary)

I took delivery of one kayak on a cold December morning. According to all reports, this boat had poor initial but good secondary stability. The summer before, a 10-minute test paddle of this model under ideal conditions had impressed me. Once I owned the kayak, however, I found my comfort level in it wasn't great, so I took it out to challenge the wake from one of the large BC ferries. Although I stayed upright, I still had no great trust in the boat. In January, we rented the Ladysmith pool for a practice session and I found out how unstable it really was. It was a beautiful looking kayak but I put it up for sale not long after that pool session.

I fell in love with another make and model that I tried out one very windy day. This new boat was a real joy to manoeuvre until I went downwind and found that it wouldn't track straight. Even with the rudder down, tracking was poor. I would have bought this model after my test paddle if it hadn't been for the poor downwind tracking. If I hadn't tested the boat in the wind I might have made another pricey mistake.

Another boat I owned was great, except to look at. The bow was anything but graceful but it cut nicely through the waves and gave a good ride. I thought the boat's appearance would grow on me, but after six months, I ended up selling it because I could never really enjoy the look of the bow.

By now you may have guessed that I'm a bit of a kayak junkie. Every fall or winter, I buy a kayak when prices are low, and during the following summer, I sell one of my older ones. It's a way to really get to know the different makes and models but not the most cost-efficient form of test paddling.

BUYING A NEW KAYAK

There are many advantages to buying a new kayak. You aren't limited to choosing the makes and models on the used market, you can choose the colours and options you want and the boat will come with a warranty. The disadvantages include paying about $400 to $1,000 more, paying GST and PST and having to wait for your boat to be built (unless you buy off the rack).

Hard chine kayaks are gaining in popularity.

Buying

You should also consider construction techniques and design. Larger manufacturers, for instance, can afford vacuum-bag technology, where vacuum pressure, or suction, is used to draw the resin through the fibreglass or Kevlar matting. This creates a lighter boat with the same strength as one made the traditional way. Many companies have also recessed the deck fittings. Although this looks nice, it weakens the boat and makes it trickier to clean.

Most manufacturers' catalogues describe the type of person and type of paddling each model is designed for, along with its handling characteristics. Also listed are specifications for weight, length, width, depth and volume. Once you decide on a boat, or at least narrow the choices down, test paddling is a must. Many dealers and manufacturers have demo boats or agreements with rental outfits to encourage test paddling. (See Test Paddling, page 21)

A Current Designs worker attends to the final details.

Some manufacturers offer a variety of additional options, depending on the model. Options may include a compass (page 133), choice of seats, thigh braces (two small wings that protrude into the cockpit just below the rim and above the paddler's thighs), an under-deck bag (above your knees), a day hatch (for lunch and rain gear) and soft deck fittings. Rudders, rudder controls (pedal type) and skegs may also be options. Some manufacturers offer customized construction, with extra fibreglass, Kevlar or graphite reinforcements. You can have the forward bulkhead moved toward the bow to accommodate a taller person or toward the stern to create more cargo space for a shorter person.

Kayaks become very personal. Buying one made just for you, with your chosen array of options, can give you a greater sense of paddling pride and ownership.

Manufacturers

The four largest kayak manufacturers on Canada's west coast are Current Designs (www.cdkayak.com), Necky (www.necky.com),

Composite kayaks are hand constructed.

Nimbus (www.nimbuskayaks.com) and Seaward Kayaks (www.seawardkayaks.com). Both Current Designs and Seaward are on Vancouver Island and seem most popular with Island paddlers. Necky and Nimbus appear to be favoured on the mainland side of Georgia Strait.

In the last few years, many smaller manufacturers have sprung up, including Atlantis Kayaks, Extreme Interface, Pacific Kayaks, Pathfinder and Teeka Kayaks. Others, such as Feathercraft, Klepper, FoldingCraft and Folbot, construct folding kayaks that can be carried as luggage, so you can take them just about anywhere. There are also a host of companies that make wooden kayaks and kits, including Pygmy Boats and Waters Dancing.

In the northwest US, some of the larger companies are Boreal Design, Easy Rider, Eddyline, Mariner Kayaks, Northwest Kayaks and Prijon. Numerous smaller ones exist, as well. Most kayak manufacturers can easily be found on the Internet.

Our experiences (Gary)

We've owned boats of many different makes, models and types. I recently built my first skin kayak. It weighs 14.5 kg (32 lb) and is easy to carry to the beach but lacks comfort and speed. My next skin model will be an improved version but I consider these to be play boats for short paddles. Paul and I each started with a plastic boat and quickly moved up to fibreglass. Now we've made the jump to Kevlar and we appreciate the few kilos that this expensive matting saves.

Neither Paul nor I overly enjoyed paddling the hard-chine, "stitch-and-sew" wooden boat I had for a couple of years. It was fine in calm seas and not bad in turbulent ones, but when the water was just a little rough, the boat lost its initial stability and gave a somewhat unnerving ride.

We both currently own kayaks that are 56 cm (22 in) and 61 cm (24 in) wide. The fit of the narrower boats is great, whereas the wider models are a little too roomy for good bracing. But when the weather gets windy and rough, the wide kayaks certainly offer greater stability and they hold more gear for multi-day trips.

BUYING A USED KAYAK

Buying a used kayak is easier than buying a used car because there aren't as many things to check. On the other hand, used kayaks aren't that plentiful during the summer months, so you may not have much choice. Here are a few things to check:

- Are the hatch covers easy to take off and are they waterproof? You can test them with a garden hose. Gaskets or neoprene covers provide a seal. Damaged ones can be replaced and are not too expensive but you should factor this into the price.

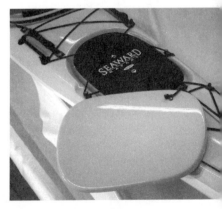

- What type of rudder system is on the boat? Does the rudder lift and re-sit easily? Is the rudder a sliding, foot-operated system or a tilt-pedal system? Check the rudder blade to see if it's bent and

Hatch covers should be watertight and easy to remove.

Foot controls for rudders can be sliding or lockout systems.

check the bracket that mounts the rudder to the kayak. If the bracket is bent, it's an indication of a mishap with something hard.

- Ultraviolet (UV) is the biggest factor causing deterioration of both rotomoulded and composite kayaks. If the kayak has suffered UV degradation, it will be easy to spot by looking for colour fade and the breakdown of neoprene hatch covers and deck shock cords. By lifting the hatch covers and comparing the colour of the deck where it was shaded by the cover to where it was not shaded, you should be able to see any damage.

- Inspect the hull and deck for cracks, gouges and scratches. Gouges and scratches are good indicators of how much and how hard a kayak has been used but cracks are more serious and may not be easily repairable. The bow and the stern should be examined for signs of hard impacts and for wear around the rudder, rudder controls and carrying handles.

- It isn't easy to determine the usage level of a second-hand kayak. Is the wear and tear an indication of normal use or an indication of abuse? One way to tell is to look at the area below the rudder pedals (or foot braces) for signs of wear. Just as a driver's foot wears the floor mat and gas pedal of a car, the paddler's feet wear this spot. You should also examine the insides of the front and rear hatches by the bulkheads. These areas are where heavy items are supposed to be stored when paddling and they will show signs of wear if the kayak has been used a lot for camping. Look at the line that raises and lowers the rudder. The wear on the last few centimetres of line near the rudder will give some indication of how many times that rudder has been up and down.

- Check the seals on bulkheads and hatches and ask if the boat leaks. You can fill the hatches partway with water and stand the boat on end to test the bulkheads. Bulkheads have an intentional pinhole to prevent potential pressurization problems.

- Ask about the kayak's age. Most fibreglass kayaks have a serial number on the hull near the rudder, which will include the date of manufacture. For instance, the last four digits in serial number QKN004890998 indicate that the boat was made in September 1998. If looked after and protected from UV, a fibreglass kayak should last 30 years. Rotomoulded boats will probably have a life-span of 10 to 15 years. If exposed to excessive UV, rotomoulded kayaks may have a lifespan as short as seven or eight years.

- You can learn more about a used kayak by looking up the model in the manufacturer's catalogue or on their web site. Dimensions, weight and volume will be given, along with a description of the types of paddling and performance intended.

Knowing what to look "at" and what to look "for" can be difficult for someone with limited kayaking experience. You may want to bring along an experienced kayaker when examining a used boat, or ask one about some of the features mentioned above, or search the Internet for specifics.

When is the best time to buy a used kayak? Generally, late summer or early fall. Many outfitters sell their stock when the season is over. Rental boats usually suffer more abuse than kayaks used for guided trips. Look on kayak web sites, and in magazine and newspaper ads.

A used single plastic sea kayak sells for $1,000 to $1,600. You'll probably pay more if the seller is including a paddle, skirt, paddle float, PFD or other accessories. If you can buy these used, you may be able to save a fair amount of money. A used single fibreglass sea kayak normally sells for $1,800 to $2,800. Double kayaks usually cost $300 to $700 more but are harder to sell. There's no tax if you buy a used kayak from an individual but buying one from an outfitter requires GST and PST.

2 Equipment choices made easier

Kayaking requires basic equipment: a paddle, PFD, sprayskirt, pump, whistle, throw bag and paddle float. In addition to these fundamentals, there are accessories such as wheels, deck bags, chart cases, etc.

Proper paddling jackets and footwear increase the paddler's comfort, and we cover these products in Chapter 4. Information on VHF radios is in Chapter 7, which deals with kayak safety. Chapter 8 is about navigation and includes information on charts, tide and current tables, compasses and global positioning system (GPS) units.

CHOOSING A PERSONAL FLOTATION DEVICE (PFD)

The Type III PFD was developed as an alternative to the bulky, uncomfortable Type I lifejacket, historically used by professional sailors to face emergency situations. The performance requirements for Type I and II lifejackets caused them to be quite bulky in front and unwieldy. As a result, many boaters were simply not wearing them.

Several changes have been made to PFDs over the past few years, including the introduction of colours in addition to the original yellow, orange and red. The changes were made because many boaters drowned while near a rescuer and not wearing their PFDs. Type III PFDs, most common among Pacific Northwest paddlers, meet a minimum requirement of 15 lb (67 N) of buoyancy.

A side-zipper PFD with whistle.

Equipment

This will keep your head well above water.

Type IV PFDs are inflatable, and Type V is a special use vest/suit. Neither are commonly used by kayakers.

Choosing a PFD

When purchasing a PFD, ensure it meets these basic requirements:
- The jacket remains approximately 5 cm (2 in) above the sprayskirt and does not ride up.
- Your arms/armpits do not chafe.
- It is easily adjustable and you are able to take it off and put it on in your kayak while on the water.
- It is designed to be highly visible in the water.
- It has enough pockets to meet your paddling needs.
- It is durable.

Coast Guard approved

Buyers may also consider style or appearance and whether the PFD is approved by the country in which you live. Canadians can be fined for not wearing a PFD approved by the Canadian Coast Guard, Department of Fisheries and Oceans, or Transport Canada.

Washington State requires all kayakers to have one Type I, II, III or V PFD per person in the kayak. If you have a Type V you must be wearing it. More information can be found at www.boatwashington.org/lifejacket.htm.

Design, size and shape

Kayak PFDs are cut shorter than ones for boating or canoeing. In many basic models, such as Buoy-O-Boy, the bottom section of the jacket flips up. Jackets vary in size from extra small to extra, extra large. Check the vest for your weight and size. Many manufacturers provide a table of information for their products. You can check the size of the PFD for weight, chest or bust size, waist, inseam, hips, sleeve and height.

Kayak PFDs have generously cut armholes to allow maximum paddling movement. Serratus (www.serratus.com), a BC company, makes PFDs with higher-placed foam, so as not to interfere with kayak cockpits. Many

This pullover-style PFD is compact but lacks pockets.

companies have a whole range of PFDs. Salus (www.salusmarine.com), an Ontario company, produces a line of kayak vests. Their Darwin and Gjoa vests are made with breathable mesh liners and a tough, 500-denier Cordura shell. One model is a kayak guide vest with additional straps, quick-release buckles and belt tunnels. It also accommodates such add-on accessories as a towline and a shoulder strobe light.

Having a front zipper or an easily reached side zipper allows the wearer to take a PFD off quickly, with minimum side-to-side movement, in order to add or shed a layer of clothing mid-paddle.

Quick release PFDs are favoured by kayaking guides.

Adjustment straps that are easily accessible in the most awkward situation are another good feature. Ideally, you should be able to release or tighten side and shoulder straps with little effort.

Visibility should win out over appearance. No one wants to be a bump in the water on a foggy day or a night paddle. Safety is the primary concern. The colour of your jacket should contrast against the colour of local waters. Many manufacturers attach reflective tape to shoulder straps and across the back and front.

Pockets and attachments

There are stories of kayakers swept from their boats in storms. The water is cold, the weather is rough, and it's difficult to get back into the boat, so the victim reaches for the VHF radio only to find that it's locked away in the cockpit. "Where's my VHF?" may have been some poor paddler's last words, uttered under the storm's downpour or across the swelling, white-capped waves. Items stored in a PFD are quickly accessible and may save your life. A number of smaller

Optional rear PFD pocket.

objects can be kept there for safety and convenience, including VHF radio, whistle, gloves, flares, knife and compass. Your pocket preferences will vary according to the amount of equipment you carry; too

Equipment

much gear, however, could affect PFD flotation or interfere with your ability to paddle.

The optional pocket hydration system is great for summer paddling.

Durability

The durability of a PFD may be an issue for some people. The strength or weight of the material will likely affect the cost. A heavy, 500-denier nylon will cost more than a lighter, 210-denier stock. The Locean PFD, made by Lotus Designs (www.lotusdesigns.com), has a 500-denier Cordura body and has been known to stand up to endless hours of wear and sunlight. Many other companies, such as Canadian manufacturer Buoy-O-Boy (www.buoy-o-boy.com), now also construct their PFDs with a 500-denier Cordura body.

Inflatable PFDs

Inflatable PFDs (Type IV) are either manual or automatic. The buoyancy standard for inflatables is 22.5 lb (100 N). The buoyancy comes from an inflatable chamber that is typically worn deflated and folded. The deflated PFD is smaller than a jacket-style PFD and does not compromise comfort. A manual can be inflated in less than five seconds, by pulling on a tab. An automatic inflatable is triggered when the PFD is immersed in water. However, exposure to high humidity or to high splashes or waves over your kayak may also cause it to inflate.

The inflatable PFD may be worn only by individuals over the age of 16 and must always be accompanied by a good, unpunctured cartridge or else be worn fully inflated. The inflatable can be used for flat-water paddling but not whitewater.

Inflatable PFDs are becoming more popular, due to their comfort and lack of bulk. They vary in price from $120 to $240.

Children's PFDs

Children under 1.5 m (5 ft) tall and 45 kg (100 lb) should not be equipped with a women's or adult PFD. When choosing a PFD for a child, fit is most important. Too often, children wear loose-fitting jackets that may come off during an emergency. Salus Nimbus, a children's vest designed to hug small bodies, is soft to the touch, encouraging children to wear it for longer periods.

Children's PFDs come in three weight sizes and often have a crotch strap. For the purpose of PFD selection, the weight of your child should include any paddling gear and clothing. A child wearing a diaper, for instance, can quickly gain up to 2 kg (4.4 lb) of extra weight, if a capsize occurs. Children who are big-boned and have low body fat may need additional flotation. Be sure to test the PFD in the water, while the child is wearing it, to ensure that the jacket will not come off and that it has adequate buoyancy.

How to care for your PFD

A well-cared-for PFD will last longer. The flotation in a modern PFD consists of closed-cell ethylene foam designed for low water absorbency and high buoyancy. Foam can compress and lose its properties. It's not recommended for use as a cushion or pillow. Here is a list of dos and don'ts:

Paul outfitted for a leisurely paddle.

Equipment

- Don't crush your PFD by kneeling or sitting on it.
- Do air-dry the PFD before storage.
- Don't expose it to direct heat from a dryer or heater or leave it in the sun for prolonged periods.
- Do rinse your PFD in fresh water, after each kayaking trip and before storing.
- Do check your PFD for rips, holes and tears.
- Do test your PFD once or twice a season for buoyancy.
- Do test the buoyancy of your PFD with the additional items you are storing in it.
- Do wash your PFD in warm water with a gentle soap.
- Do discard old PFDs by cutting them up and disposing of the pieces (this prevents someone from re-using a sub-standard one).

What do I buy?

Your first concern may be cost. There are several entry-level jackets that are reasonably comfortable and inexpensive. Expect to pay $60 to $120. Add pockets and more adjustment points and the cost increases.

The next price range falls between $120 and $160. These jackets come with additional features, such as special

Front-zipped PFDs are easy to put on and take off while in your kayak.

pockets, or they are designed for better arm movement, or have neck holes that ensure greater mobility.

Kokatat (www.kokatat.com) makes a PFD designed to fit a woman's shape, in the $120 to $140 range. Peter Harris, a long-time paddling enthusiast and owner of the Vancouver Island Canoe and Kayak Centre in Victoria, says women's PFDs have become very popular. Even men are choosing them because they are very adjustable and comfortable.

In choosing a PFD, check to see if it's approved. You may end up being the unlucky one to pay a fine. Try the vest on carefully. Sit down in a kayak with a paddle and test the PFD. Look for freedom of movement, riding up (this happens a lot), snugness and ease of adjustment. Try different types of strokes, and check for chafing and any restrictions to your paddle stroke.

Our experiences (Paul)

When I first chose a personal flotation device for kayaking, I pulled out an old orange lifejacket I had used for sailing. On my first trip, my arms chafed a little against the armholes and the top of the jacket rode around my nose. Over the years, we have seen many instances of PFDs riding so high they cover the paddler's head.

Gary and I quickly upgraded to what most of the outfitters were buying for their customers: a basic Serratus kayaking PFD. A few years later, we upgraded to a similar style with more pockets. Since PFDs are always improving, we've upgraded again to get more compact and stylish PFDs.

Our wives both own women's Kokatat PFDs and love the fit.

BUYING THE RIGHT PADDLE

Most people buy their first kayak paddle when they buy their first kayak. If that kayak happened to be used, chances are the paddle was thrown in as part of the deal. When buying a new kayak for the first time, it's often the salesperson who helps the customer choose a paddle.

Gary enjoys his lightweight graphite paddle.

Equipment

Wood paddles won't chill your hands on cold days.

Paddles are classed as whitewater or touring. As this book is about sea kayaking, we'll assume that touring is your intended usage. The four variables are length, blade size, blade shape and material type. The benefits of specialty paddles will be covered later in this chapter.

Considerations

- paddle length
- blade shape
- blade size
- materials
- paddle shafts
- specialty paddles

Paddle length

Paddles are measured in centimetres from blade tip to blade tip. The normal range is 215 to 245 cm (85 to 96 in) but some manufacturers produce paddles as short as 203 cm (80 in) and as long as 274 cm (108 in). You can custom order any length, within reason.

The basic principle is: the taller you are, the longer the paddle.

Even more important for determining paddle length is the width of the kayak. A 215-cm (85-in) paddle used in a wide double would be a joke, as you could barely reach the water with it. It could be a good length, however, for a tall person in a narrow kayak.

The other factor determining length is the angle of your paddle stroke. Some people prefer a very vertical stroke and would need a shorter paddle. Most of us tilt our paddle at about 45 degrees and, therefore, need a bit more length.

Confused? If you are a beginner, under 1.8 m (5 ft 9 in) tall and paddle a boat about 60 cm (24 in) wide, a 225- to 235-cm (88- to 93-in) paddle would probably be a good choice. Try before you buy. Make sure the different lengths you try all have the same blade size and shape, or you won't know whether it's the blade or the length that makes one feel better than another.

Blade shape

Most blades are asymmetrical. They are designed to be in the water at an angle but the submerged surface areas on either side of the shaft need to be equal. This prevents the paddle from twisting as you pull it through the water.

Unfortunately, not all your paddling energy propels the kayak forward. Your paddle's entry into and exit from the water—and those pesky little whirlpools that spin off your blade—can all waste energy. Good paddle design and a proper paddle stroke will minimize these losses.

The shape of the blade's face and back has a strong effect on performance. Power dihedral and soft dihedral designs both have advantages. A dihedral angle is one where two planes intersect. The term is mostly used in the aeronautics industry to describe how air

---

BLADE SHAPES

Quill-shaped   **Touring**   **Touring with bent shaft**

travels above and below a wing to give lift. In the paddle manufacturing industry, a power dihedral refers to a blade with a very slightly cupped face. This gives maximum power, torque and acceleration. The soft dihedral is just the opposite of a cupped face; the two sides are flared back. The result is better directional control and a smoother, flutter-free performance.

Quill-shaped paddles are designed to dig below turbulent water.

Blade size

Traditionally, touring blades are small and long. A small blade weighs less than a large blade and takes less work to pull through the water. The experts will tell you that a large blade isn't good for touring. To some extent, we agree, but if you pace yourself, a large blade can offer some advantages. Most people we paddle with use larger blades than the experts recommend.

Touring blades come in various sizes and shapes.

A couple of advantages of large blades are ease of bracing and an increased ability to power stroke out of danger. If a whirlpool the length of a kayak opens up in front of you, you'll be thankful for a larger blade. The disadvantages of large blades are additional weight and greater wind resistance.

The blade sizes of our two favourite paddles are 18 by 47 cm (7 by 18.5 in) and 18 by 46 cm (7 by 18 in). These are considered large blades. A small blade might be 13 by 46 cm (5 by 18 in). The numbers don't look that different but there's quite a difference in performance. Longer blades (quill-shaped) usually measure around 11 by 61 cm (4.5 by 24 in). They're designed to dig deeper into the water, below the sometimes-turbulent surface. They give better leverage but require more skill to use.

Gary's Grey Owl paddle still looks new after years of use.

Materials

Blades are made from wood, plastic, fibreglass and graphite (carbon). Wood and plastic are similar in weight. The buoyancy of wood makes it come out of the water nicely. Plastic blades are affordable and durable, which makes them popular with outfitters. Plastic blades are made thicker, to resist warping, and often weigh 30 percent more than similar fibreglass blades. Fibreglass blades are more expensive but often are better designed.

The lightest material is graphite, which is 25 percent lighter than fibreglass, but a graphite paddle can cost twice as much as fibreglass. Graphite is strong but not nearly as durable as plastic. "No digging for clams or log rolling!" said the Nimbus Paddles rep, when extolling the company's graphite blades. Our graphite paddles have met a few barnacle-covered rocks and been thrust into the shell-covered bottom while turning in a shallow river mouth, yet they still look new. Some people, however, put their pricey graphite paddles to near-industrial uses, which is asking for trouble.

Paddle shafts

Paddle shafts are made from fibreglass, graphite, wood and aluminum. Flexibility and warmth are important. Wood has both. Fibreglass is the most common material used and is also both warm and flexible. Graphite is the lightest shaft material but very rigid. Ideally, a shaft should have a bit of flexibility, as it makes your paddle strokes a little smoother and easier on your own moving parts. Aluminum is cold and not great for northern climates. It also adds

Bent shaft paddles offer better wrist ergonomics.

Equipment

about 50 g (1.75 oz) of weight to the paddle. Shafts should not be perfectly round. A very slight oval shape helps you grip the shaft better and keeps the blades angled properly. Shaft diameters can vary: too large is hard for small hands to grip, too small can cause hand cramps.

Specialty paddles

There are a few paddles on the market with very different styles. One of these is the bent-shaft paddle made by Current Designs. It's available with several blade models. The shaft is bent at eight degrees where the paddler grips it. This causes less strain on the paddler's wrists and is a good design for expedition touring.

Many racing paddles have bent shafts, too. However, they also have spoon-shaped blades. A racing paddle is great if you're in a hurry but it can quickly tire you out, and the blade shape is a poor design for bracing.

Winged paddles are a cross between touring and racing paddles. The top edge of the blade has a small ridge or wing for grabbing more water. Winged paddles require the use of a more vertical paddle stroke and are also poor for bracing. Nimbus may have solved the bracing problem with its Feather model. This paddle blade has a normal back but a semi-winged front. For some, this represents the best of both worlds.

For those who want to try different paddle lengths and feathering angles, there are models available with adjustable fittings on the shaft. Loosen the fittings and you can make the shaft longer or shorter. The same fittings allow you to feather the blades to any angle.

The last specialty paddle we'll mention is the Greenland paddle. It's an old design that's gaining in popularity. The Greenland paddle has a long narrow blade that starts close to where the paddler grips the shaft. The area of blade surface in the water is the same as, or greater than, that of a conventional touring paddle. The blade is only about 10 cm (4 in) wide, which allows the paddler to grip the entire blade when rolling the kayak. The Greenland is a light paddle that pulls through the water easily and allows for hours of paddling with

very little fatigue. Bracing ability, however, may not be nearly as good as with a conventional paddle.

Specifications

Most paddle manufacturers include information on sizing range, available formats, blade-angle position, blade dimension and paddle weight. Sizing range indicates the lengths available, often in 5- or 10-cm (2- to 4-in) increments. Paddles can come in one, two and four-piece formats. Most are two-piece, for easier storage. A one-piece paddle is stronger and lighter but more difficult to fit in your vehicle. A four-piece paddle is small enough, when broken down, to fit in a kayak hatch.

Blade-angle positions can be feathered and unfeathered. Most ocean kayakers have their blades unfeathered, meaning that the two blades are in the same plane. Whitewater kayakers feather their blades either 45 or 60 degrees (and some paddles can be feathered 75 degrees). In whitewater kayaking, both paddle and paddler are often under water and only one blade should be in the power position. By having the blades feathered, when one blade is angled for the stroke, the other is angled to slice easily through the water. In ocean kayaking, a paddle can be feathered for kayaking against strong winds. This will allow the blade that is being pushed forward through the air to have minimal wind resistance, as its face will be parallel to the water surface. The downside of feathered blades is that they tend to stress the paddler's wrists.

Paddle weight is a very important factor, as several hours of paddling requires a lot of paddle strokes. In one day, you might make 20,000 strokes. Even though the difference between a light paddle and a heavy one may be only 300 g (10.5 oz), this can make a big difference. Normally, manufacturers will list the weight of a 225- or 230-cm (88- or 90-in) paddle. Longer paddles weigh marginally more, usually about 20 g (0.7 oz) for every extra 10 cm (4 in) of length. Lightweight graphite paddles are godsends for older paddlers, children and those suffering shoulder, elbow or wrist problems.

Spare paddles

A good safety rule is that every group of kayakers should carry at least one spare paddle. There are some very low-end paddles, for as little as $60. A much wiser option, though, is to buy a good wooden paddle for about $150. Having two differently shaped paddles on

Equipment

your trip will allow you to trade off, depending on the state of the weather and your physical condition.

Manufacturers

Aqua-Bound Technology Ltd. (www.aquabound.com) and Nimbus Paddles (www.nimbuspaddles.com) capture the lion's share of sales on the West Coast. Current Designs (www.cdkayak.com) produces paddles that are very popular with Northwest kayakers. Mountain Equipment Co-op (www.mec.ca/paddling) sells their own brand of touring paddles, as well as Nimbus and Grey Owl paddles (www.greyowlpaddles.com). These paddle makers and others can be found through www.easykayaker.com.

There are many manufacturers and models to choose from.

Prices

Paddles are not cheap. If you want a paddle that's strong, light-weight, well-engineered and designed, you'll pay dearly for it. A decent wooden or plastic paddle costs around $150. A fibreglass model is about $200 and a graphite one will usually cost between $300 and $400. It's a lot of money, but once you've used a good paddle, you won't want to go back to a cheap one.

Our experiences (Gary)

My first kayak was a short double that I planned to paddle with my wife, Teesh, or daughter, Katherine. The salesperson looked at me, told me I had fairly big shoulders and recommended a long paddle with a large blade. As my wife and daughter are both much smaller than I am, he suggested shorter paddles with smaller blades for them. Fortunately, he knew his stuff and his recommendations have served us quite well.

They were good products but our needs changed and I've since sold both paddles. Kayaking was taking up a serious portion of our recreational time and we wanted higher-end models.

As we advanced from a double to several single kayaks, our needs changed again. I found a used 215-cm (85-in) graphite paddle for my daughter that was as light as a feather. She was 12 at the time, and about 30 kg (65 lb); this paddle was ideal for her.

My second single kayak was wood. I was one boat richer and one paddle short. I naturally felt that a wood paddle would be an appropriate choice. Fortunately, our favourite salesperson/outfitter/guide was willing to sell me his well-worn personal paddle, which just happened to be made of wood.

From a kayak you gain a unique perspective on the world.

This poor beat-up paddle had a lot of strokes to its credit and really looked it. I sanded it down, refinished it and fell in love with wood paddles. I eventually sold it with the kayak but bought a new Grey Owl Sirocco wood paddle. Many of my paddling partners have this same model.

I found out how tough my Grey Owl was one day as I darted between the pilings under a dock. I was moving at a good clip and angled my paddle to miss the pilings. I didn't angle enough, though, and the leading blade caught the piling on my left. Then the trailing blade caught the piling on the right. The paddle bent for a brief moment but didn't break, and I came to an abrupt stop. As the paddle straightened, the kayak was propelled backwards and I had much of the air knocked out of me. My Grey Owl still looks almost new, despite the abuse it has seen over the last five years. The resin-

Equipment

capped blades are really tough, even against barnacle-covered rocks.

At the Vancouver Island Paddlefest in Ladysmith, I finally bought my dream paddle: a graphite Wavewalker from Nimbus. Was it justifiable to spend that extra money for a really good paddle? Yes, and since then, I've enjoyed many hours of paddling with this beauty.

Each specialty paddle has its own merits and and can be a good choice, but not for everyone. Paul and I have each owned a bent-shaft graphite paddle but I still like the conventional designs best. Most of our paddling is done with 230- to 240-cm (90- to 95-in) large-bladed graphite paddles.

SPRAYSKIRTS

Sprayskirts are essential pieces of safety equipment that prevent your cockpit from filling with water, keep you dry and warm, and protect you from UV rays. Some companies manufacture a halfskirt that allows for air circulation but shields you from splashes and sunburn.

A sprayskirt is an essential piece of kayaking equipment.

Sprayskirts must not only maintain a secure seal but should also come off easily, should you capsize and need to wet-exit. They must be equipped with a grab loop to facilitate a quick release. Sprayskirts (sometimes called skirts or spray decks) are sized by cockpit dimension and some are also sized by waist circumference. The sprayskirt manufacturer or retailer can usually recommend the correct size for the make and model of your kayak.

Sprayskirts are constructed in three basic styles: all nylon, all neoprene or a neoprene deck attached to a nylon waist tunnel. The nylon in the skirt is typically coated with polyurethane for waterproofing. Most nylon skirts have a drawcord at the chest and shoulder straps. Sprayskirts range from $30 to $60 for nylon and $100 to $200 for neoprene and nylon/neoprene.

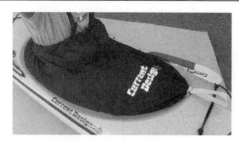

It is important to leave the front grab loop accessible.

All nylon

Nylon is much lighter than neoprene and has different properties that affect safety and comfort. Because nylon does not stretch, the fit across the coaming of your cockpit has to be snug. A nylon skirt is more prone than a neoprene skirt to being dislodged by a strong wave, which could result in your cockpit filling with water. The advantages of a nylon skirt include lower cost, lighter weight, less bulk, and more comfort and coolness in warm weather.

All neoprene

Neoprene, a more elastic material, stretches easily over the coaming and its flexibility promotes safety. The all-neoprene skirt has been largely used in whitewater and surf kayaking applications. The snug fit around the waist and coaming keeps water out when large waves wash over the kayak and during rolling and bracing. Neoprene also helps protect paddlers from the cold. The tautness of the neoprene at the waist may be mildly uncomfortable for sea touring, especially over long distances.

Neoprene skirt options include a fitted or adjustable waist; some skirts even come with a water-resistant zipper. An adjustable waist

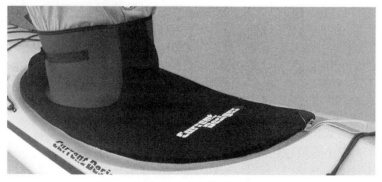

Neoprene sprayskirts will keep you warmer and dryer.

Equipment

has a number of advantages. People of different sizes can use the skirt and those with changing waistlines may find it more suitable. A fitted waist provides more comfort and warmth and can help hold the sprayskirt at the correct height without shoulder straps. A zippered neoprene skirt has an additional advantage: with one quick motion, you have access to your cockpit and the items stored there.

Nylon/neoprene

The combination of nylon and neoprene gives the best of two worlds: the comfort, ventilation and lightness of a nylon tunnel and the taut surface and flexibility of a neoprene deck. Eliminating leakage at the seams has been a challenge when joining the two different materials. The touring skirt from Brooks, for example, uses a neoprene tube to join the nylon tunnel to the neoprene deck. In other designs, the seams have been moved away from wave and spray areas to help minimize leaks.

A sprayskirt should be fitted so that the transition between tunnel and deck is a little above waist level; this can be accomplished more easily with shoulder straps, which hold the tunnel at the correct height. If the skirt is worn too low, an indentation will form while paddling and often fill with water, compounding the problem of leakage at the seam connecting tunnel to deck. Even neoprene

Comfort and flexibility are combined in the nylon/neoprene sprayskirt.

sprayskirts will eventually leak at this seam, if worn too low.

The neoprene/nylon skirt works well in most weather conditions. If you are going to buy only one skirt, a nylon/neoprene model may be the best choice. It will keep you dry, reasonably well vented and comfortable for most types of paddling.

Shoulder straps

The main disadvantage of a skirt with shoulder straps is the difficulty of removing or putting on clothing while in the kayak. Partway through a paddle, the sun often comes out or disappears and some clothing adjustments are necessary. Most companies now make skirts with quick-release shoulder straps.

Our experiences (Paul)

There are times when I forgo the use of a sprayskirt and simply enjoy the sensation of water dropping from my paddle onto my legs. My skirt, however, will always be folded neatly and be easily accessible under the bungee cords. On a warm, windless day, my only concern is getting sunburned across the front of my legs. However, when I gather my equipment for a day of paddling or a longer trip, I'm well aware of the importance of the sprayskirt.

Although we have all three types of skirts, it's usually the nylon/neoprene strapless model that we choose. Whatever choice you make, don't forget to leave your quick-release loop out, in order to be able to easily and quickly pull the sprayskirt off the coaming, should you capsize.

SAFETY EQUIPMENT

In addition to PFDs and sprayskirts, basic safety equipment includes rescue devices, paddle leashes, signalling devices and bailers.

Rescue devices (paddle floats $35 to $130, throw bags $20 to $60)

A paddle float is used for self-rescue. As the name implies, it's a flotation device that attaches to the blade of your paddle, in order to allow the paddle to be used as an outrigger pontoon while performing a wet-entry. The most common paddle float consists of a fabric-covered piece of Styrofoam, complete with buckle, strap and blade pocket for quick attachment to your paddle. Natural West Coast Adventure Gear (www.kayak.bc.ca) makes one of the nicest ones.

Paddle floats should be easy to attach.

Equipment

When shopping for a paddle float, look at buoyancy and attachment. Some foam paddle floats do not offer enough buoyancy for a large person and there is no standard for this type of device. Attachment to the paddle needs to be easy, as you will likely need to do this under difficult conditions.

We don't recommend inflatable paddle floats, as hypothermia can set in quickly. Having to blow up a paddle float

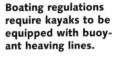

Boating regulations require kayaks to be equipped with buoyant heaving lines.

in high waves while submersed in cold water adds too much delay and stress to the situation.

For those who want versatility, a paddle float that converts to a beach seat and backrest is available from Natural West Coast Adventure Gear. Seaward makes a kayak seat bottom that is also a paddle float. We've seen homemade paddle floats constructed from old PFDs, foam blocks, duct tape and bungee cords. When carrying any type of float, make sure it's attached to your kayak so, if you capsize, you don't have to let go of the boat to retrieve the float. This can be a fatal problem, as a person in the water wearing a PFD often can't swim fast enough to catch up with a wind-driven kayak.

Some kayakers don't have enough upper body strength left, after hours of paddling, to do a wet-entry. If this might be a concern for you, carry a stirrup. The stirrup is a rope tied in a loop and used in addition to a paddle float. It can be looped around the cockpit coaming so that it hangs low enough in the water to provide a foothold. The rope is usually about 3 m (10 ft) long but this measurement is dependant on the kayak and the size of the paddler. A stirrup should be tested and adjusted during a practice session.

Another rescue device is a buoyant heaving line, usually referred to as a throw bag. Canadian and US regulations require all boats to carry one and it must be at least 15 m (50 ft) in length. This device is thrown to someone in trouble to assist in a rescue or provide a tow. In reality, you can't throw very far while sitting in a kayak. Some kayakers make their own heaving line from a small beachcombed float and a length of buoyant rope.

Paddle leashes ($10 to $20)

Although the purpose of a paddle leash is to prevent losing your paddle in the event of a capsize, it also provides the convenience of not having to balance or secure your paddle whenever you want two hands free. Many experienced paddlers who are proficient at the Eskimo roll, however, don't use paddle leashes.

You can easily make one using a short piece of small-diameter bungee cord and a small plastic clip. You want a paddle leash to be lightweight. There's no sense spending an extra $100 on a graphite paddle and then hanging a heavy leash on it. The nicest leash we've used came from Scotty (www.scotty.com). It has swivels at both ends; the cord is a spiral type (like a telephone handset cord); there's a clip on one end for attaching to the kayak and on the other end is a tight-fitting rubber ring for the paddle. It comes with an extra rubber ring for your spare paddle.

Paddle leashes offer additional safety and convenience.

Signalling devices ($1 to $5)

Kayaks must be equipped with a sound-signalling device, such as a whistle or air horn. In the case of kayaks, a whistle makes more sense. Most of us can shout fairly loudly but that might change if we are suddenly submersed in cold water. All paddlers should carry a whistle attached to their PFD that they can sound without detaching. Many PFDs are sold with a whistle on a leash. Scotty makes a boating whistle with a clip-on attachment.

Whistles are inexpensive, so buy a good one, as it could save your life. Most paddling groups have a prearranged set of whistle signals. Typical is:
- one whistle blast, all come and help
- two blasts, all stop paddling and wait

A whistle might save your life.

Bailing devices ($30 to $50)

Required by boating regulations, a bailer can be a hand scoop, bucket or pump. Although a few kayakers go the cheap route and use a sour cream container as a bailer, most buy a pump. The pump should have brightly coloured positive flotation and be long enough to reach over the coaming. Scotty manufactures 35-cm (13.5-in) and 46-cm (18-in) models. The shorter one works for most single kayaks but the taller model is often needed for doubles.

KAYAK NAVIGATION LIGHTS

In Canada, kayaks not over 6 m (19.5 ft) in length must have a navigation light if the craft is operated before sunrise, after sunset or in low-visibility conditions. The minimum requirement is a watertight flashlight. For kayaks 6 to 8 m (19.5 to 26 ft) in length (usually doubles), six approved Type A, B or C flares are also required. American regulations are similar: navigation lights with a visibility range of 2 nautical miles are required on kayaks under 7 m (23 ft) in length from sunset to sunrise. In order not to become a speed bump, you may wish to have better equipment than this minimum standard.

Paddling in the early morning, as the sun streaks across the ocean, or in late evening, as remnants of light dance through coastal fir and arbutus, captures the very heart of kayaking. Full-moon paddles are

Without a good navigation light, you are virtually undetectable in fog or at night.

wonderful. The wind may be no more than a light sea breeze while the still waters reflect a clear image of a setting sun or an orange moon. Night settles in and you head home in the darkness.

Without a good navigation light, you are virtually undetectable to a motorized craft. The skippers of large powerboats navigated from a high console have difficulty seeing you, given their angle of view. Lee Hindrichs reported a sad story in the April/May 1999 issue of *WaveLength* magazine. Three people (a husband, wife and male friend) were returning from a local pub to a waterfront home when the worst possible nightmare happened. Paddling in a high traffic area in Sproat Lake Narrows, they saw a powerboat approaching at an estimated speed of 30 km/h (20 mph). It is not clear from the article whether the three people had night lights, but if they did, the lights were obviously not clearly visible. The three paddlers waved their paddles frantically and screamed. The boat struck the woman's kayak, shattering it, knocking her unconscious, and causing the two men to capsize. Later, it was discovered she had sunk 40 m (130 ft) to the bottom. Although the men tried to find her, with no light their efforts were in vain. The woman was not wearing a PFD; if she had been she might have survived with only a concussion.

It's always wise to paddle with at least one other person. Nighttime paddling is safest with a group. A group's lights often include flashlights, headlamps, flashers, glowsticks and commercial navigation lights. Having a variety of lights makes the group much easier to see. What, though, is the best equipment to have while paddling in darkness or restricted visibility?

This light attaches to the kayak using a suction cup.

Navigation light options

Many commercial products are available. The simplest and most affordable is a watertight flashlight. It can also be used for other activities, such as finding your tent after dark. Even if you choose a more sophisticated navigational light, we recommend you also carry a flashlight, as a backup, to shine at approaching boats. Floating flashlights are available at most hardware stores by brands such as Coleman. A good waterproof flashlight can start at $16. Scotty (www.scotty.com) manufactures a watertight flashlight, as well as a portable running light, that can be mounted or attached to a kayak.

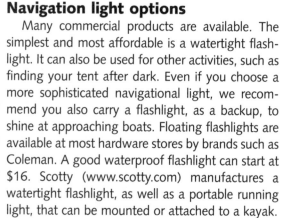

Equipment

Scotty's mountable light fits into a Scotty fishing-rod holder and has an overall height of 70 cm (28 in). The rod holder should be bolted onto the kayak, where it won't interfere with a wet-entry. The light uses two D-cell batteries and turns on by twisting the lens. Our favourite light, also manufactured by Scotty, fits into a rubber suction-cup mount that sticks to the kayak and also attaches to a bungee cord. It's about 20 cm (8 in) high. This light could sit anywhere on your craft but is best toward the rear. If mounted too close to you, your body may limit its visibility. The rod holder unit costs approximately $70 and the smaller suction cup unit is about $50. The light has a 360-degree lens that is visible from 2 km (1.2 mi) away, if the kayaker's body isn't in the way. Scotty's rod-mounted light can be seen even more easily because of its 70 cm (28 in) height.

Other products include a flashing Novlab Lazer Stik that is waterproof and highly visible and a Wildwasser Guardian light. A small flasher mini-light by Pelican (www.pelican.com), attachable to your PFD, is a good low-cost solution. The ACR C-Strobe lifejacket light (www.acr-electronics.com) is waterproof, has a lightweight design and a visibility of up to 3.2 km (2 mi).

Reflective tape on your PFD and paddle increases your visibility in the water. Newer PFDs sport reflective tape in key areas such as the shoulders and back. We both have reflective tape mounted on the shafts of our paddles. Additional tape can be added to your PFD.

A headlamp allows you to quickly direct your light toward an approaching watercraft.

Your decision about a light should consider how the light affects or interferes with your vision and that of your fellow paddlers. If you are paddling to enjoy the full moon, the experience will be spoiled if your buddy's light blinds you. But safety is the most important consideration. It's worth spending a little extra to have more than the minimum.

Regulations

Canada and the US have the same regulations regarding lights.

This is an excerpt from the *Canadian Collision Regulations*:

"A vessel under oars may exhibit the lights prescribed in this Rule for sailing vessels, but if she does not, she shall have ready at hand an electric torch or lighted lantern showing a white light which shall be exhibited in sufficient time to prevent collision."

Our experiences (Paul)

We enjoy summertime full-moon paddles. Usually, we paddle into the sunset and return facing the rising moon. Several times, we have paddled on moonless nights when returning from Ladysmith's fireworks show at Transfer Beach. We stick close to shore, away from the boating channels. It's hard to see rocks, and wakes from passing boats often hit without warning.

Gary and I each have short Scotty suction-cup mounted lights and are amazed how far the light is visible. Gary often wears a red bicycle-type flasher clipped to the front of his PFD.

MISCELLANEOUS EQUIPMENT

In addition to basic safety and navigational paddling equipment, there's a whole realm of goodies out there to improve your paddling comfort and fun. Take a walk through one of the larger kayak or outdoor shops and you'll be amazed. Here are some products worth considering.

Dry bags keep sleeping bags, clothing and food dry.

Equipment

Deck bags ($30 to $100)

These are meant to be secured to the kayak's deck and give quick access to things such as binoculars, cameras, sunglasses, snacks, sunscreen, lip balm, etc. They limit the amount of free deck space for charts and safety gear, however, and also offer some wind resistance. You can make an inexpensive deck bag by using a fanny pack.

Under-deck bags ($40 to $50)

Used like a deck bag, these net-like receptacles are located above your knees in an out-of-the-way location and can be used both as a bag and a shelf. The downside to under-deck bags is that you have to release your sprayskirt to reach them and they often require drilling holes in the deck of your kayak for mounting.

Drybags ($10 to $50)

Even though hatches are usually watertight, everything that isn't waterproof in your kayak should still be protected. Garbage bags work but they puncture easily and don't make much of a fashion statement. Most kayakers use drybags

Deck bags are convenient but can create wind resistance.

for packing clothes, sleeping bags and other items that need to stay dry. These come in various sizes, colours and materials. They seal by rolling the mouth of the bag closed and buckling it into a handle shape. Clear bags make it easier to find things such as your missing sock but they don't hold up as well as the coloured ones. Most are made of polyvinyl chloride (PVC) or a similar material and can be difficult to stuff sleeping bags into because of surface friction. Natural West Coast Adventure Gear (www.kayak.bc.ca) makes four different sizes of drybags using 210-denier coated nylon fabric.

As storage space in a kayak can be at a premium, some manufacturers produce tapered bags that fit the shape of kayak holds.

Clear dry bags make it easier to find things but have a shorter lifespan.

Cockpit covers ($30 to $40)

A cockpit cover, usually made of nylon, will keep leaves, insects and dust out of your kayak when in storage and will reduce the amount of rainwater that gets in during transport or lunch on the beach. The cover has an elasticized cord sewn around the edge that fits over the cockpit coaming. Water can puddle on the cover and may slowly leak through. When camping, we store our paddles, PFDs and sprayskirts, etc., in the cockpit and then put the cockpit cover on overnight. When paddling, it is stored behind the seat. Covers can blow off during transport, so it's advisable to secure them to a deck bungee.

Painter line ($10)

A painter line is an adjustable line that attaches to the bow of your kayak. It can be used for walking your boat through shallow water. By attaching a spring line just behind the cockpit, it's also possible to walk your boat from shore against a fast current. While camping, kayaks stored on the beach should always be tied to something solid during the night and a painter line works well for this.

Towline ($50 to $70)

Sometimes, due to fatigue, illness or injury, a fellow paddler may need to be towed.

Towing may be required to help an ill, injured or tired kayaker

Although a throw bag or painter line might do the trick, these lines can interfere with the rudder of the towing boat and may be hard to release quickly, if trouble arises. Ideally, the towline should connect to a belt on the towing paddler's waist and have a quick release feature. Towlines are fairly simple to make using 15 m (50 ft) of 6-mm (0.25-in) floating polypropylene line and some plastic fittings.

Foam pads and seat cushions ($4 to $25)

You can buy peel-and-stick foam pads for padding the bottom, sides and back of your seat. The pads are also available for thigh areas. They provide comfort and a small degree of warmth. Kayakers sometimes use self-inflating seat cushions, but stability can be compromised. By raising the seat 25 mm (1 in), up to 60 percent of stability can be lost. When shopping for a seat cushion, try to find one that provides comfort without too much thickness.

Wheels ($80 to $140)

A cart or set of wheels works well for walking your kayak down a boat ramp or onto a ferry. These devices can be quickly and easily disassembled and packed into the kayak until the return trip.

A cart consists of two wheels and a lightweight padded frame. It is placed under the kayak's cockpit and the kayak is strapped to it. The advantage of a cart is that it supports most of the kayak's weight and tends to stay in place more easily than a stern-wheel set. The disadvantage is that it will take up more space in your kayak.

Stern wheels look a bit like a pair of bicycle training wheels. They have a small V-shaped frame that fits under the stern of the kayak and are held in place with straps. They weigh less than a cart, cost less and will fit through a hatch without disassembling but they don't stay in place as well as a cart.

Wheels work well for walking your kayak down a boat ramp or onto a ferry.

We have made transporters from old golf carts and with lawn-mower wheels. These homemade vehicles will help move a kayak when you don't happen to have two adults handy (if you're paddling a double with a child in the front, for instance). After getting the kayak to the water, the cart can be stored in your vehicle.

Hats ($5 to $100)

Hats are necessary for UV and rain protection and for warmth. For summer paddling, you want a hat that won't cause overheating. Ideally, hats should be comfortable, ultra-lightweight and secure, even in a gale-force wind. For a number of years, Tilley Endurables (www.tilley.com) was the leader in providing these qualities but there are now more brands and styles. Outdoor Research's Sahale

Sombrero (www.orgear.com) is popular with kayakers. Expect to pay at least $60 for a really good all-in-one hat.

Protector cases ($10 to $150)

Cameras, cell phones, radios and other electronic gear need protection from the marine environment. Soft, waterproof "see-thru" and "talk-thru" cases are available in many sizes for cell phones and VHF radios. Hard-shell cases can be even better at providing protection. Pelican (www.pelican.com) makes a line of foam-core gasketed cases with automatic pressure purge valves. The foam comes in pull-apart blocks, allowing you to create padded, custom-fit cavities for your equipment.

Rigged for sailing.

Sails ($200 up)

Sailing a kayak can be a lot of fun, and it can also be dangerous. Stability can be an issue, and if you capsize, your kayak can go sailing off without you. We heard of this happening several years ago; the kayak was found 8 km (5 mi) away from the kayaker, who died of hypothermia. Sails are available in various rigs: one style employs two masts in a V-shape; another, in a more traditional style, uses a single mast with twin outriggers for extra stability.

Kayaks don't tack very well, so you are mostly limited to a downwind sailing adventure. The trip back can sometimes be a long paddle.

Equipment

3 Transporting, care and maintenance

ROOF RACKS AND FOAM BLOCKS

Often the hardest part of your kayaking journey is getting the kayaks on the vehicle, tying them down and then getting them off and down to the water. The cost of a new kayak certainly justifies protecting it during transport. Although foam blocks will suffice in many cases, a roof-rack system is easier to use and normally more secure. A well-constructed, secure roof-rack system will not only protect your kayak and vehicle from damage but will make loading quicker and easier.

The roof rack truly is a system. The first component is the part that attaches to the vehicle, either using roof rails, door or gutter clips, or bolts. Uprights, or towers, are held in place by these attachments and

A homemade padded rack allows a custom fit.

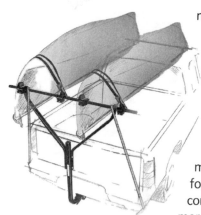

may contain locking mechanisms to guard against theft. The structural part of the rack system normally consists of crossbars or load bars. These are held off the roof by the towers. Finally, saddles, rollers and/or posts are added to give proper surfaces to rest the kayak.

Roof-rack systems vary from home-made wood or metal racks padded with foam to expensive, accessory-loaded commercial systems that may be worth more than the vehicle under them. Each system has its advantages and disadvantages.

A trailer-hitch mount works well for pickup trucks and cars with small roofs.

The bottom line, however, is preventing your kayak from falling or shooting off the vehicle like a torpedo onto hard pavement (and this has happened too many times).

Driving down the highway at 110 km/h (70 mph) against a 25-km/h (15-mph) headwind subjects a kayak to hurricane-force winds. Travelling more than 100 km (62 mi) of potholed logging roads to reach a destination like Bamfield will cause pounding and other stresses to a kayak. What the kayak sits on, how you position it, what you use to tie or strap it down and how tightly you secure it all have a bearing on whether or not damage will occur.

Types of roof racks

- foam blocks
- custom-made (homemade)
- OEM (Original Equipment Manufacturer) factory-installed
- specialized

Foam blocks

A pair of foam blocks can be purchased from most kayak shops for approximately $25. The blocks are roughly contoured to the shape of a kayak hull and made to fit a number of different-shaped crossbars (rectangular, circular, flat). The foam block is usually pushed onto the crossbar and is held in place by the weight of a kayak sitting on it.

Foam blocks can be used without a rack by placing them directly

Transport & care

on the roof of the car. The greatest difficulty with this method is tying or strapping the kayak in place. When using foam blocks without a rack, people tend to tie the kayak to the vehicle's bumpers, which can stress the boat's backbone.

The main advantage of the foam-block system is cost—they're cheap! The blocks can fit on your existing roof rack, so you don't have to buy additional accessories such as saddles or rollers.

A foam-block system is easy to install but it's not overly secure. The blocks move and can come off, unless taped to the rack or otherwise secured. If you have several thousand dollars' worth of kayaks on your roof, you might want to consider investing in a better rack system.

Custom-made (homemade) roof racks

Custom-made (homemade) roof racks are commonly made of wood but can be made from metal and are usually designed to carry two or three kayaks.

A wooden homemade roof rack bolted to a truck canopy.

The advantages of custom-made racks include saving money and coming up with a design that fits your situation. Pickup trucks, with or without canopies, are often well-served by multi-purpose, custom-built racks. These can be as strong as commercially installed roof racks but may not be as easy to use or as streamlined or attractive.

In designing a custom-made rack, the most difficult aspect is the attachment to the vehicle. Often, holes are drilled and the rack is bolted through the roof of the vehicle or canopy, using urethane caulking to maintain a watertight seal. In designing your rack system, first see if the width of your vehicle will accommodate the number of kayaks you want to carry. In designing a rack, try to minimize air resistance in order to preserve fuel economy. Racks and lines that whistle or hum when travelling can be a real nuisance. If racks stick out beyond the vehicle, they may injure people.

Consider overall height, too, both with and without kayaks. Height can be a problem in parking garages and on ferries. BC Ferries has a height surcharge that kicks in at 207 cm (6 ft 8 in) or 213 cm (7 ft) and ranges from $20 to $130, depending on the route. Information on height and fares is available at www.bcferries.com

OEM (Original Equipment Manufacturer) factory-installed racks

Many vans and sport utility vehicles are sold with OEM (original equipment manufacturer) roof racks. A number of passenger car models also have OEM racks. Normally, the side portions (tracks or rails) of these racks are quite reliable. The crosspieces, on the other hand, are often constructed from plastic and may not be structurally sound enough to carry kayaks.

Commercial roof-rack manufacturers have systems to fit virtually all OEM racks. The accessories will strengthen or improve the OEM system. It's wise to consult a rack manufacturer before placing kayaks on an existing OEM system or ordering an OEM rack from the car dealership.

Specialized roof racks

Commercial roof racks vary in price from $250 to $1,000 or more, depending on the accessories. Canadian Tire and other large automotive stores sell multi-purpose roof racks along with accessories for transporting kayaks. A generic commercial brand, however, could end up scratching or denting your vehicle and may not fit as well as a high-end system.

There are a number of specialized rack manufacturers, including Yakima (www.yakima.com) and Thule (www.thuleracks.com).

Various tower types and heights are available.

Transport & care

These companies allow you to build the rack of your choice for the make, model and year of your vehicle.

A specialized system allows for design of a roof rack to match the customer's needs and consists of towers, clips or tracks, crossbars, lock cores, a kayak mounting system and straps. The mounting system is what the kayak sits on. Additional accessories, such as a boat loader or lock cables, can also be purchased.

The tower can be mounted on virtually any vehicle, with or without rain gutters. If your vehicle has factory-installed rails or tracks, the towers can be attached to them. If not, gutter attachments or clips are used. These are specially designed to make the tower fit your vehicle like a glove.

There are several types of towers, which vary in height and in how they attach to the vehicle. There are side-mounting towers for campers and canopies and there is even one that bolts through the roof of the vehicle. There's also a rear rack system that fits a 5 cm (2

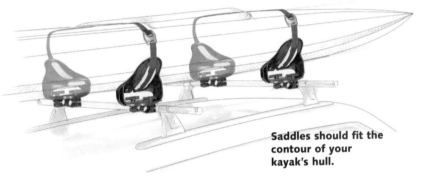

Saddles should fit the contour of your kayak's hull.

in) trailer-hitch receptacle. This is a good option for pickup trucks.

For those vehicles that don't have factory-installed rails or tracks, and whose owners don't want to drill holes in the roof, the best option is to use clips. The clips attach to the rain gutters or door jamb, and as long as the owner drives with the doors closed, they work well.

Crossbars are the backbone of the roof-rack system and come in varying lengths. They may be round, square, curved or flat. Kayak mounting components (saddles) attach to the crossbars and often the tie-downs do, as well.

The choice of kayak mounting system is the most critical decision in the purchase of roof racks. Saddles or rollers that fit the hull are used for mounting kayaks in an upright position (as when the kayak is in the water). Each kayak requires four saddles or two saddles and two rollers. There are several types of saddle mounts available from the large manufacturers. The saddles should contour-fit your kayak's hull, gripping it firmly, yet allowing the boat to slide smoothly. The saddle should be fairly wide, in order to maximize the surface support area and distribute the load.

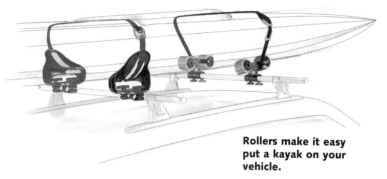

Rollers make it easy put a kayak on your vehicle.

In some cases, rollers can be installed on the rear crossbar, in place of a saddle. Some rollers pivot to allow an easy dismount of your kayak. There are also rollers that mount behind the rear saddle for easy loading. These are excellent systems. The decision to install saddles or rollers or both will depend on the type of vehicle and whether you want to load and unload the kayak by yourself.

Stackers or posts are available for mounting kayaks on edge. This usually requires padding the crossbars. Some stackers hold the kayaks on edge, but not quite vertical, which places less stress on

A stacker system increases the number of kayaks that a vehicle can carry.

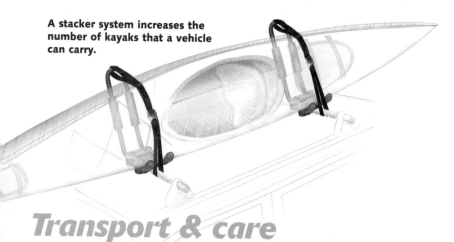

Transport & care

them. The value of stackers is twofold: you can load more than two boats on one rack system and your kayaks will be less prone to damage from rough roads.

A base rack (includes crossbars, towers and locking system) costs around $300. Saddles are about $200 per kayak. Installation and additional accessories add to the price. Dealers know which system will work best with your particular vehicle and type of kayak.

A specialized commercial roof-rack system is a luxury compared to a homemade set-up or foam blocks. Two big bonuses with commercial racks, though, are peace of mind and ease of use. A specialized rack can be the answer for those who want to load and unload by themselves. Because any specialized system will be fitted to your particular vehicle, it's less likely that the rack will cause scratches or dents.

Tips for transporting kayaks

Kayaks should be supported at or near the bulkheads, since this is the boat's area of maximum strength. Sea kayak bulkheads are normally about 1.5 m (5 ft) apart. This means that the distance between your crossbars should be from 1.2 to 1.8 m (4 to 6 ft).

Plastic (rotomoulded) kayaks on roof racks are susceptible to "oil-canning." This describes the large dents that may be created on hot days, if the kayaks are not properly supported at the bulkheads. Fortunately, plastic remembers its original shape and these dents can

A kayak should be supported at or near the bulkheads.

usually be repaired with a little application of heat and pressure.

Kayaks should be gently strapped or tied down near the bulkheads. Overtightening places extra stress on them. Use straps with buckle guards (available from Yakima or Thule) or soft, high-quality rope. Marine supply stores are good sources for soft rope. For a second level of security, bows and sterns can also be tied, but these ropes should only be semi-tight so as not to stress the kayak's backbone.

When tying bows and sterns, the rope should first be attached to the car. Then the running end of the rope should be tied to the kayak. This way, any extra rope is kept well away from the vehicle's wheels. There have been cases of knots coming loose and rope passing under a tire, causing massive damage to the kayak. Having the extra rope with the kayak, instead of near the vehicle's bumper, will help prevent this.

Kayaks left on top of vehicles can fill with water during heavy rain, and the extra weight can stress a kayak. We've heard of one case where the owner drove over a curb with a large amount of water in a kayak and cracked it. Using a cockpit cover will help keep rainwater out but many covers are not completely waterproof and tend to puddle and sag. If you drive with a cockpit cover in place, be sure to secure it to a bungee cord, as covers have a bad habit of blowing off.

Kayaks are often longer than the vehicle they are riding on, so a red flag at the stern may be required by law and for general safety. Take care to park so that the projecting stern is not in the way of passing cars or pedestrians. We have heard sad stories of kayaks being backed into immovable objects and meeting low ceilings in parking garages.

Our experiences (Paul)

Gary started with foam blocks on the roof of his car. Occasionally, the foam blocks stayed on the roof after the kayaks went into storage. Then Gary would drive off and lose them at the side of the road. Amazingly, we always found them later that day or soon after. He quickly progressed to using the blocks on a $40 roof rack but they would shift when we went downhill on steep, bumpy roads. Ducttaping the blocks to the rack helped solve that problem but the setup was far from perfect. We've seen many funky rack systems in our time, even ones using pillows.

We have built a number of homemade racks for various vehicles. My pickup truck has both a steel rack with wooden crossbars/saddles and wooden racks that are bolted onto my canopy (see photo on page 61). The wooden racks were sanded and urethaned, and

Transport & care

had holes drilled for tie-downs. The saddles were custom-shaped to the hulls and covered with thin foam to cushion the kayaks and provide a non-abrasive surface.

Gary custom-built wooden racks to fit his 4Runner. They were attached by drilling through the roof and using galvanized carriage bolts. Over several years, he has modified the design to make loading and tying down easier. His most recent version is made from red and yellow cedar and holds two kayaks on flat and a third one on edge. A pool noodle (a child's swimming aid) was cut into two pieces and had a light rope threaded through its centre. The noodle is fastened around the middle kayak for cushioning when three boats are loaded on the rack. The rack is padded with pipe insulation foam glued in place with contact cement (see photo on page 59).

CARE AND MAINTENANCE OF YOUR KAYAK

Most new kayaks come with an owner's manual that includes guidelines for care and maintenance. Fortunately, kayaks require little of either. If you bought a used kayak, you can often access the manufacturer's guidelines via the Internet. Care and maintenance mainly consist of cleaning, lubricating moving parts and tightening loose fittings. Composite kayaks will benefit from waxing at least yearly.

You should wax your composite kayak at least once a year.

Check and tighten all fittings occasionally.

Kayaks are made from different materials: fibreglass, Kevlar, polyethylene, wood and fabric (skin-on-frame and folding kayaks). Care and maintenance, with minor variations, is pretty much the same for all types. Here are some basic tips and suggestions:

• Salt corrodes metal fittings. After each use wash your kayak with fresh water. A gentle car soap may also be used.

• Check all screws, nuts and fittings for tightness every few months.

• Store your kayak on fitted, padded rests that are placed close to the bulkheads. Your kayak can lose its shape if left lying on a flat or rugged surface.

• UV destroys plastic and fibreglass. Keep your kayak out of the sun during storage. Protect it by applying a UV coating (303 Aerospace Protectant or similar product).

• Inspect your kayak for wear and tear. Examine components that could break (buckles, lines, cables, shock cords, neoprene hatch covers or hatch gaskets, etc.). Replace anything that is beginning to wear. Make sure neoprene hatch covers are in good shape. Never paddle a boat without watertight hatch covers unless it has tapered buoyancy air bags.

• Inspect the spring that locks the paddles together.

• Check your foot braces or sliders for wear.

• Inspect your rudder or skeg control. Use silicone spray instead of oil for lubrication, as sand tends to stick to oiled surfaces.

• DO NOT drag your boat on the beach. Do not sit on the hatch or deck when the kayak is out of the water.

• When car-topping, tie ropes or straps tightly across the kayak but allow bow and stern tie-downs to be slightly loose. Do not let the boat fill with rain and then drive over rough terrain. Be very careful that the bowline doesn't come loose and get caught under a wheel (see Transporting your kayak, page 66). Use soft ropes or straps with buckle guards to tie your boat to the roof rack.

- Fully loaded kayaks should not be carried only by the handles. They should also be supported with a hand under the keel, as too much stress on the carrying handles could damage the deck or cause a handle to break.

Support a loaded kayak with a hand under the keel.

- Fibreglass kayaks should be treated with a boat-cleaning or polishing wax compound at least once a year. Not only will your kayak look better, it will glide through the water much more easily.

KAYAK REPAIR

Since kayaks are made from a variety of materials, it would take an entire book to discuss all the different repairs that might be needed. The following is a brief guide on how to fix the more common problems.

Replacements for worn or damaged fittings and components, such as rudders, seats, hatch covers, shock cords, handles, etc., can be bought from most dealers. Manufacturers and dealers often offer repair services for those who don't want to do their own work or if the damage is more serious.

Repairing rotomoulded kayaks

Scratches on rotomoulded (plastic) boats can be removed with heat, using a wide-tipped blowtorch or an electric iron. This may be best done by an expert. If you want to try it yourself, practise on a plastic bucket first. Damaged hulls can be heat-welded by a plastic-kayak manufacturer. We've heard of a plastic kayak being heat-welded on a small island, using a campfire and a plastic bucket found on the beach. It was an emergency situation and was good enough to get the paddler home.

Plastic kayaks will become brittle with age and UV exposure. Once this occurs, not much can be done to reverse the deterioration.

Repairing composite kayaks

Composite (fibreglass) kayaks are very repairable. Before attempting any repairs, however, visit your bookstore or library and read up on working with fibreglass and gel coat. There are many good books on the subject, and "how-to" information is available at most marine suppliers and plastics shops. Fortunately, these materials are quite easy to work with and require few tools.

For faded fibreglass boats, a good cut-polishing often brings the colour back. Make sure you treat the boat with a UV protective coating afterward. Boats that need more than just polishing can be painted with fibreglass paint or gel coat. For best results, have this done by an autobody shop.

Small cans of coloured gel coat to match your boat can be bought from the kayak manufacturer or from marine repair shops. Catalyst, fibreglass and resin are available from marine suppliers and plastics shops. Wet sanding paper up to 2000 grit is available at many automotive and marine supply stores.

The following guidelines are for minor repairs. Always clean the area to be worked on with soap and water first and then let it dry.

Transport & care

MARKS ON THE FINISH THAT WON'T WASH OFF

1. Use a one-step fibreglass cleaner/polish/wax. This should remove the marks.
2. Let dry and then buff with a soft cloth.

DULL OR FADED FINISHES

1. Treat entire surface area with a fibreglass finish restorer (303 Aerospace Protectant or similar product).
2. If finish is not restored, rub area with a fibreglass rubbing compound using a soft cloth and short strokes. Keep turning the cloth as more rubbing compound is applied. Be aware that the outer surface of the gel coat is being removed; you don't want to go too deep with this treatment.
3. Once scratches are rubbed out, apply one-step fibreglass cleaner/polish/wax.
4. Let dry and then buff with a soft cloth.
5. Apply UV protectant.

MINOR SCRATCHES

1. Gently rub area with a fibreglass rubbing compound using a soft cloth and short strokes. Keep turning the cloth as more rubbing compound is applied. Be aware that the outer surface of the gel coat is being removed; you don't want to go too deep with this treatment.

Lubricate moving parts with silicone spray.

2. Once scratches are rubbed out, apply one-step fibreglass cleaner/polish/wax.
3. Let dry and then buff with a soft cloth. Apply UV protectant.

GOUGES, DEEP SCRATCHES, WORN SPOTS AND HOLES IN THE GEL COAT

1. Rough up the damaged area with 80-grit sandpaper to create a good bond (do not rough a larger area than necessary).
2. Mix a bit more gel coat and catalyst than you think you might need, following the instructions on the catalyst (normally about eight drops of catalyst per teaspoon of gel coat).
3. Apply mixed gel coat with a small brush, putty knife or popsicle

stick and feather the edges (apply the gel coat more thinly at the edges and extend it past the damaged area). The application should be a bit proud of the surrounding surface (slightly raised, so you can sand it down). Working time should be about 15 to 20 minutes in a warm environment. Pop any air bubbles.

4. Let dry and then sand with 220-grit paper.
5. Repeat, if necessary.
6. Once gel-coat applications are complete, sand with 220 grit then wet-sand with 400 grit and 600 grit.
7. Treat with rubbing compound as described above.
8. Apply one-step fibreglass cleaner/polish/wax and buff.
9. Apply UV protectant.

LARGE-AREA GEL-COAT REPAIRS

1. Sand with 220-grit paper and feather edge of repair area.
2. Clean away sanding dust.
3. Mix gel coat and catalyst.
4. Apply gel-coat mixture over repair area using a spray gun (you will need to clean the gun fairly quickly after spraying).
5. Repeat, if necessary.
6. Once gel-coat applications are complete, sand with 220 grit then wet-sand with 400 grit and 600 grit.
7. Treat with rubbing compound, as described above.
8. Apply one-step fibreglass cleaner/polish/wax and buff.
9. Apply UV protectant.

HOLES, CRACKS AND BADLY WORN AREAS

These repairs must maintain the structural strength of the kayak and are best left to fibreglass professionals. Fibreglass cloth and resin will require an artistic touch to prevent a lumpy, patched look and excessive increase in weight. Even kayaks broken in two can be repaired so that the damage isn't apparent from the exterior. Kayak manufacturers and marine repair shops are the best choice for repairing holes, cracks and badly worn areas.

Our experiences (Gary)

We usually do a major once-over of our boats every spring, checking all fittings, touching up gel-coat damage, lubricating moving parts and applying a coat of wax. We replace bungees when they

Transport & care

One of those unforgettable moments.

start to fray or lose their elasticity. Mid-season, after a few major trips, we again wax the hulls, as there is a big performance gain from doing this. At the same time, we use 303 on the decks for appearance purposes and to protect against fading. I've seen some pretty sad-looking kayaks that weren't very old.

When it comes to repair work, I've been amazed at what the professionals can do. One person I know lost a kayak from a trailer on the freeway. It collided with a chain-link fence, breaking in two. In another case, a kayak was stolen and abandoned on a rocky West Coast beach and was pounded by the winter surf for more than a week. It was still in one piece but there wasn't an area larger than a sand dollar that was unblemished. In both cases, the boats were repaired at the manufacturer's factory and came out looking new (but slightly heavier).

4 Apparel choices made easier

PADDLING FOOTWEAR

Whether you rent a kayak, own one, kayak with outfitters or go on self-guided trips, you will need proper paddling footwear. The right footwear will protect you from barnacles, sharp broken shells or jagged rocks when launching and landing. It will keep your feet warm and dry in winter and allow them to breathe and be comfortable in summer.

Is there one right choice? No. But there are numerous affordable, well-made products available. Here are the pros and cons for each type:

Types of footwear
- sandals
- aquasocks and aquashoes
- runners
- neoprene booties
- waterproof socks

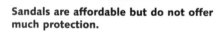

Sandals ($10 and up)

Sandals are affordable but do not offer much protection.

Recommendations:
- choose sandals with good fit and ankle support
- avoid leather

Pros:
- affordable
- allow feet to breathe and stay dry
- can be used with waterproof or neoprene socks
- acceptable for beachcombing and short hikes
- good for hot weather paddling

Apparel

Cons:
- don't offer much protection from rocks, shells and other sharp objects
- very cold in winter
- sand and small bits of shell can get between sandal and skin, causing irritation
- can catch on rudder pedals
- heel and side of foot can rub inside kayak, causing irritation

Aquasocks and aquashoes ($5 and up)
Recommendations:
- require a good fit, not too tight or too loose
- choose units with thicker soles
- great to have along after paddling and for swimming and camping

Pros:
- affordable
- allow feet to breathe a little and maybe stay dry while paddling
- acceptable for beachcombing and short hikes
- good for hot weather
- lightweight

Low-cut neoprene booties are easy to put on.

Cons:
- don't offer much protection from rocks, shells and other sharp objects
- very cold in winter
- sand and small bits of shell can get between aquasock and skin, causing irritation

Runners ($20 and up; runners designed for paddling $65 and up)
Recommendations:
- avoid leather
- runners designed for paddling are preferable
- choose buckles or Velcro, rather than laces

Pros:
- multi-purpose
- good for beachcombing and hikes
  - good for warmer weather when neoprene booties may be too hot
    Cons:
    - don't offer ankle protection from rocks, shells and other sharp objects
      - sand and small bits of shell can get in runner and cause irritation

Neoprene booties ($30 and up)

Recommendations:
- kayak booties are preferable to dive booties
- ones with good soles are best, if you want to do minor hiking
- booties with zippers are much easier to put on and take off
- height and liner type have a strong impact on warmth

Pros:
- offer good protection
- provide some warmth for feet while paddling
- acceptable for beachcombing and very short hikes

Cons:
- don't allow feet to dry
- very cold to put on, if still wet
- somewhat expensive but will last many years if looked after
  - require washing or rinsing after each use in saltwater; may smell due to bacteria

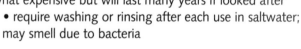

Waterproof socks ($35 and up)

Recommendations:
- taller models, ideally mid-calf or higher (38 cm or 15 in), are preferable
  - thin, waterproof socks will fit inside booties but neoprene socks may be too thick

Apparel

Pros:
- feet stay dry
- can be worn with other footwear

Cons:
- expensive
- feet can't breathe

Recommendations (Gary)

So what is the right footwear for you? First, decide whether you want to paddle just during warm weather or if you want to extend the paddling season. Next, how much pad-dling are you going to do? Your metab-olism and circulation also enter the equation: Do you get cold feet easily or tend to overheat?

For those who want to paddle at least six months of the year, or plan to make kayaking part of their year-round recreational activities, I suggest pur-chasing a pair of zippered neoprene paddling booties. Two West Coast com-panies with great paddling booties are Whites and Brooks. A third outfit, Mountain Equipment Co-op, sells booties under its own brand name. My wife, daughter and I have booties from all three sources and recommend all three companies highly.

There are several styles of booties. The types of soles vary; some have heat-

A warm choice for winter paddling.

reflecting liners that are claimed to increase warmth by up to 40 per-cent. Tall booties are too warm for most people during much of the year, but if your feet get cold easily, this may be the way to go. Paul and I find a good compromise by wearing ankle-height booties and tall, waterproof Sealskin socks during the colder seasons. (No baby seals were killed to make these socks; Sealskin is the brand name.) Hot water from a thermos can be used to pre-warm cold booties, though you should use caution as the water can sometimes be a little too hot.

Manufacturers are creating hybrids of these products. Whites makes a titanium-plush-lined, Tundra-zippered boot from 7-mm (0.28-in) neoprene that has a durable, ribbed sole with a moulded toe and heel cap. Whites also produces a 3-mm (0.12-in) neoprene Roc Sock, a lined warm sock with a durable, rubber outer sole that offers protection from sharp objects and holds up well to wear and tear.

Brooks manufactures a 6-mm (0.24-in) zippered bootie with a plush interior. It also makes a model called the Amphibian boot. This is a bit of a cross between a runner and a bootie, and offers warmth, ruggedness and comfort. If you're looking for a very tall waterproof boot, their 7-mm (0.28-in) Kamit model reaches almost to the knee, allowing you to wade fairly deep and stay dry.

Both Whites (www.whitespaddlesports.com) and Brooks (www. brookspaddlegear.com) are manufacturers; they have links on their web sites to local dealers. Two other notable US manufacturers are Teva (www.teva.com) and Five-Ten (www.fiveten.com).

Mountain Equipment Co-op in Canada (www.mec.ca) and Recreational Equipment Incorporated in the US (www.rei.com) both offer a full line of paddling footwear. You can find product information on-line from both companies.

Some of the lower-priced neoprene footwear is made in China and is usually labelled accordingly. Other products are labelled

When fog descends it's a good time to take a break.

Apparel

"semi-dry," meaning they are not 100 percent waterproof. For some people, these issues are not important.

All footwear, but especially neoprene-constructed designs, should be rinsed in clean fresh water after use in salt water or the swimming pool. Zip booties up after washing, while they dry. Bacteria or mould on the neoprene can cause the booties to smell. Soaking them in a product such as Mirazyme, available from most dive shops and paddling stores, will usually deodorize them.

For warm-weather day paddles with reasonably good launching and landing spots, sandals can be an acceptable solution. Aquasocks are also fine in these conditions.

Although I know a few people who wear gumboots for winter paddling, this can be a dangerous practice, as gumboots are difficult to swim in and heavy when full of water.

If you plan to do a lot of kayaking, you will most likely end up with an assortment of paddling footwear to suit the various types of trips you take and the weather you will encounter.

Our experiences (Gary)

My introduction to kayaking and to paddling footwear was with an outfitter. Like most outfitters, he supplied his clients with a list of what to bring. Footwear was listed and there was a strong warning associated with it: we would not be allowed to wear flip-flop thongs as these were "PRECURSORS TO SPRAINED ANKLES OR WORSE!" This was written in bold capitals, and as these were the only bold capitals (and only exclamation point) on the list, I figured our outfitter was somewhat emotional about this point, perhaps with good reason.

So what to wear on my size 8 feet? According to the list, if I planned to paddle more than once, I should invest in a pair of neoprene zippered booties. Otherwise, I could bring aquasocks, sandals with good ankle supports or a second pair of runners for paddling.

Being somewhere between frugal and cheap, I opted for aquasocks. Later, I paid for my decision by losing a bit of skin while launching in knee-deep water where the bottom consisted of deceptive, seaweed-covered shells and jagged rocks. Even on a nice beach launch, aquasocks weren't ideal. I tended to pick up bits of sand and shell between my feet and the footwear, which led to rubbing and raw spots by the end of the two-day trip.

Not long after, I purchased my first kayak but was still without acceptable footwear. I'd been using aquasocks and sandals but had no protection for my ankles. My skin toughened and the sand problem mostly disappeared but barnacles and other sharp shells could still do damage. Finally, about a year later in Mexico, I walked into a dive shop and tried out my 30-year-old high-school Spanish. My Spanish left lots to be desired but I left with a pair of zippered neoprene booties that are still in use today, despite being re-glued several times. For a guy who disdains yuppie sportswear, I now have almost every type of paddling footwear available.

PADDLING CLOTHING

Overview (Paul)

My first paddling jacket was a raincoat. I'd just purchased a second-hand kayak and didn't have the cash to buy paddling gear. The raincoat material was heavy and the arm movements stiff but at least it was waterproof. The raincoat wasn't cut right in the arms for pad-

dling and it tended to ride up from my sprayskirt. Looking for more comfort, I purchased my first splash jacket about a year later.

Paddling jackets are designed for a variety of purposes and conditions. Jackets are generally termed splash, semi-drytop and drytop. They aren't cheap, and finding the right one for your needs requires a bit of thought. Normally, drier models tend to be warmer—often too warm for summer paddling. However, if you plan to paddle in conditions where waves may roll over you, there's a lot to be said for a semi-dry or drytop. If rain and an occasional splash from a wave is all you need to deal with, then the basic splash jacket type will probably meet your needs. The best of all worlds is to own all three types.

Choosing the right paddling top is important for comfort and dryness.

For those who need extra protection from the cold, a wetsuit can be a good solution. It can be worn as your main garment or underneath a paddling jacket, for more warmth. Other forms of paddling underwear, such as fuzzy rubber and water-resistant fabrics, can also be worn in layers, to provide comfort. Through experience, we have found layering to be the best option in most circumstances.

Apparel

Products
- splash jackets ($65 to $200)
- semi-drytops ($100 to $300)
- drytops ($200 to $600)
- wetsuits ($70 to $150)
- paddling underwear ($40 to $100)
- paddling pogies and gloves ($15 to $40)

Materials
Nylon, neoprene, four-way stretch polyester, fuzzy rubber, Lycra, imitation silk fabrics, Velcro, urethane, Gore-Tex, silicone, Tectron DWR

Splash jackets
The splash jacket is usually a basic nylon shell and may have a number of features that provide varying levels of comfort and protection. These include adjustable closures at the neck and cuff, and a drawstring at the waist. The splash jacket can be bought long-sleeved or short-sleeved. Splash jackets are laminated or coated with products such as Gore-Tex, polyurethane or silicone. Another method of water-

A short-sleeved splash jacket offers basic comfort and protection.

proofing involves a lightweight polyester membrane sewn between the lining and the outer shell.

Semi-drytops
Some companies, such as BC-based Navarro, use the term semi-drytop. The idea is to have some of the waterproof protection of a drytop but to retain the versatility and light weight of a splash jacket. Many semi-drytops have two layers for most of the body area. The layers are joined at breast height but are separate at the waist. The inside layer is designed to go under your sprayskirt while the outside layer goes over it. This layering is known as a "tunnel." It protects against leakage at the waist area, if a large wave washes over you and your boat.

We noted small differences between the semi-dry and dry styles. The semi-dry jackets, for instance, have smaller neoprene waistbands and do not achieve the zero tolerance for water penetration at the wrist, neck and waist that the drytops manage. Material weight is not as heavy as a drytop.

Drytops

A drytop is exactly what it says it is: water should not get past the wrist, neck or waist openings, fabric or seams. The construction of drytops varies from manufacturer to manufacturer in the key areas of neck and cuff design, waist design, elbows, bulk-saving features and seams. If you are going to spend the money for a drytop, make sure you first test the suit for comfort around the neck and elbows, and for freedom of movement while paddling.

A drysuit (one-piece top and bottom) is an option, if you plan on doing really serious cold-water paddling. As with a business suit, you can buy a drysuit off the rack or have one custom-tailored. You can also go with a two-piece suit that has a separate drytop and drybottom.

Drytops are designed to keep all water out.

Whites (www.whitespaddlesports.com) manufactures a very reasonably priced drytop called the Rodeo. The neck and wrists are constructed with soft but durable latex. Gary likes the fit of his Rodeo jacket. He only wears it when kayaking in very cold weather and finds it comfortable and warm, though quite a struggle to put on and take off.

Navarro (www.navarrogear.com) manufactures several drytops, including a women's model. Navarro's drytops offer a free-moving neck construction and a double-tunnel waist that locks out water coming up the deck. Stohlquist (www.stohlquist.com) constructs

Apparel

three styles of drytops with an expansion back design to allow more movement at the shoulder blades.

Whitewater enthusiasts, surf kayakers, kayakers who love to do the Eskimo roll, and storm and cold-weather paddlers usually wear drytops. In other words, if you plan to get really wet or need lots of warmth, a drytop may be the answer. The downside of a drytop is that a good sweat can be built up in a short time. Lightweight, breathable drytops are now available but they are very expensive.

Wetsuits

What you wear under your paddling top can be almost as important as your outer layer. A wetsuit is what many paddlers choose for cold weather and added protection against hypothermia. A kayaker's wetsuit is thinner and more flexible than a diver's.

The human body loses heat from three main areas: the head and neck, the inner thighs and under the arms. Wetsuits trap a thin layer of water between skin and neoprene that your body is able to heat. The kayak wetsuit prevents evaporative heat loss while keeping you comfortable and warm. A wetsuit may prevent hypothermia, or very low body temperature, either while you are kayaking or in case you fall into the water. Check with the manufacturers on how fast hypothermia may occur with the varying thicknesses and materials of their wetsuits.

You can purchase a "farmer John," an entire suit or separate items, such as a top (short or long-sleeved), pants (full or short-legged) or shorts. (A farmer John looks a bit like bib-overalls.) There are even children's wetsuits on the market. The Tempest John from Whites is made with titanium-coated nylon and neoprene, and is 3 mm (0.12 in) thick in high-wear areas. A titanium membrane on the inside surface of a wetsuit reflects body heat inward. Zipper location is a consideration with wetsuits, as this affects how easy it is to answer the call of nature.

Paddling underwear

If conditions aren't cold enough to warrant a wetsuit, you may still need additional warmth under your paddling clothes. Paddling tops work to keep you dry but provide little insulation. Lightweight fuzzy-rubber and other high-tech, thin, stretchy, neoprene-like materials make great undershirts. They provide warmth and cushion your skin from the cold feel of the jacket material.

In warm, wet-weather paddling conditions, most people tend to sweat under their tops. A thin silk or imitation-silk shirt will absorb the moisture from your body, providing greater comfort than many other natural fibres. Unless you enjoy feeling damp, cotton fabrics are your worst choice.

A neoprene vest can be worn under paddling clothes.

Pogies and paddling gloves

A pogie wraps around your hand and attaches to the paddle shaft. It is somewhat like a glove but allows your bare hand full contact with the shaft. Pogies offer protection from water yet allow a firm grip on the paddle. Whites advertises their pogies (www.whitespaddlesports.com) as ergonomically designed to fit your hands and keep water out.

There are a number of companies that make paddling gloves. The gloves are quite thin and are generally constructed from 2- to 3-mm (0.08- to 0.12-in) neoprene. They are designed to grip a paddle with relative ease and keep your hands warm. Gloves can be stiffer and harder to wear and use than pogies but offer more warmth. Some paddling gloves are designed to provide extra flexibility. Shop around and don't buy the first pair you see.

Some paddling gloves are designed to provide extra flexibility.

Waterproofing

Clothing manufacturers have devised several systems to keep water from leaking in at the wrist, neck and waist areas. Drytops use the gasket system almost exclusively. Splash jackets and semi-drytops may have gaskets, Velcro-fastened neoprene or a combination of the two.

The gasket system, a tight-fitting rubber or latex material at the neck and cuffs, is most effective for sealing but makes the jacket more difficult to put on and take off. Also, you can't loosen the gaskets while paddling in good weather and water conditions. (The gaskets are in rings that can be cut back until you get the proper fit. Ideally, you should wear the drytop a few times to stretch the gaskets before trimming them.)

The neoprene-with-Velcro-closure system allows you to adjust the tightness of the fit. It's also possible to take the jacket off in the kayak with this system. This is convenient for those times when the rain turns to sunshine and you start to cook.

The type of coating used to protect the nylon will determine a jacket's durability and breathability. Urethane, for example, which provides most of the waterproofing on Navarro's 210-denier Oxford nylon paddling jacket, is not a breathable product. A jacket from Lotus Designs (www.lotusdesigns.com), however, also made with lightweight 210-denier nylon, is coated with Tectron DWR (Durable Water Repellent), which waterproofs but also maintains breathability. Urethane acts more like a splashguard and is durable and long-lasting. Tectron DWR, a common fluoropolymer, allows fabric to breathe but will slowly wear off. It can be reapplied by spray, however, to restore the waterproofing.

Paddling clothing should offer flexibility and stretch.

What's out there?

Whites, a BC manufacturer, produces the fleece-lined Orca paddling jacket. It has a neoprene gusset neck that folds in and can be Velcroed shut, and neoprene cuffs. This is a very competitively priced jacket.

The Action Jacket from Kokatat (www.kokatat.com) is made with a Gore-Tex laminate. Gore-Tex is still considered one of the best waterproofing products on the market because its thin porous membrane has holes large enough for breathing but too small for water droplets.

There are many excellent jackets on the market, by Canadian and US companies, but what do you buy? The choice will depend on your lifestyle, needs and budget. Often, the Canadian-made jackets sell well in the US, due to the difference in the value of the dollar. Recently, a kayaking partner bought a jacket for both hiking and kayaking. Many paddlers also hike, cycle, walk or simply enjoy standing in the rain (a likely West Coast option). Buying a jacket to suit several purposes is a practical option and helps preserve one's budget.

A tunneled semi-dry top. One layer goes over and one goes under the sprayskirt.

Excellent splash jackets are available in the $100 to $120 range. REI (www.rei.com), a US outdoor-equipment store, has a web site where you can research jacket prices. MEC, the Canadian version of REI, has a selection on its web site at www.mec.ca. Splash jackets with additional features such as Gore-Tex laminate or a more supple lining cost more.

Many jackets are designed for stormy conditions. Jesse Simpson, at Ocean River Sports in Victoria, recommends the Skanorak pullover by Lotus Designs. This breathable anorak, or hooded jacket, for ocean kayakers is constructed with water-resistant fabric and has a lifetime warranty. Kokatat also produces lines of hooded jackets made with Gore-Tex and urethane protection. NRS (www.nrstouring.com) has the SeaTour jacket, with a shock-cord waist and taped seams, at a comparatively low price.

Our experiences (Paul)

I own a Navarro basic splash jacket with a urethane coating, neoprene gusset neck and neoprene cuffs that I cinch up to keep dry. It

Apparel

meets my basic needs during a rainstorm in the summer but on a warm, wet day, the jacket does make you sweat.

Gary owns most types of paddling tops. He finds the drytop too warm for all but really cold days and the drybottoms a bit bulky. Gary recently bought a hooded, half-zipper NRS jacket that has quickly become his favourite. My wife liked it, too, and bought a full-zipper version. You don't need to remove this jacket when the sun pops out because the front and armpit zippers allow enough ventilation for moderate cooling.

We have found layers of clothing to be the best option for most paddling. By carefully choosing what to wear under your paddling jacket, it's possible to use the same jacket almost year-round.

Some humour and perspective from Gary

You may be a bit fanatical about paddling if:
- You own more paddling jackets than dress jackets
- Your wetsuit's always wet
- Your drytop's never dry

5 Food tips

Unlike backpacking, weight isn't a problem while kayaking, so meals don't have to be freeze-dried or anything too out of the ordinary. Cooking conditions may be a little primitive, but most paddlers tend to eat very well—so well, in fact, that the term "float and bloat" is often used by guides.

COOKING EQUIPMENT

Because of camping regulations or seasonal fire dangers, fires are often not allowed at campsites, so if you plan on something hot, you'll need a campstove. Even though weight may not be an issue for kayakers, size can be, so stoves should be small. Most paddlers carry a one-burner stove fuelled by propane, butane, naptha gas or other liquid fuel. Salt from the marine environment **Compact cooking** takes its toll on these stoves **equipment.** and they may last only a few years, unless wiped with oil after each trip. Stoves are available at hardware and outdoor-equipment stores and range in price from $35 to $170. Safe, compact bottles for transporting extra liquid fuel are also available.

A cooking pot with a lid that doubles as a frying pan is ideal. Handles should either lock or else allow easy pouring from both pot and pan. You can buy cookware sets with nesting pots. As you may only have one burner for cooking (although two are more useful with a group), you shouldn't need many pots.

Single burner petroleum gas stove.

MEAL PLANNING

Diet is personal but there are a few things you may want to consider. First and foremost, how much time do you want to spend

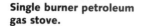

Food always tastes better when cooked outdoors.

preparing meals? On leisurely trips, meal prep and eating may be a main social event. On the other hand, if the "chief cook and bottle washer" decides that he or she wants a holiday, you may opt for quick, easy meals like bagels and cream cheese, handfuls of nuts, a beverage and a cookie or chocolate for dessert.

A combination of a few gourmet meals and some basic easy ones works best. Having some no-cook foods for lunch and breakfast will give you more time for paddling. If you're unfortunate enough to hit a patch of rainy weather, no-cook meals will also come in handy. We always take extra food and water, in case we end up staying longer. Extra food also gives us more menu options.

Our routine is to each look after our own breakfasts and lunches (though we often share) and then take turns preparing communal suppers. This works well with five people or fewer but cooking for six or more is not easy with small pots and one-burner stoves.

We buy all our food at the grocery store, instead of spending the extra money for freeze-dried backpacking or camping foods. We try to avoid bulky items. Bagels travel well. Canned foods, such as stew, make for easy meals. Fruits and fresh veggies are always a treat. Trail mix and cookies are standard operating procedure and we like to add dried fruit and Smarties to the store-bought mix. But don't let us catch anyone picking out all the Smarties.

Meal ideas

Good meals will bring a touch of comfort to your kayaking trip. Here are some general tips:

- Shop for fresh food on shorter trips (seven days or less). Your kayak has the space to hold oranges, melons, tomatoes or whatever you desire.
- Plan your menu beforehand with your friends or family. Kayak cookery is a social affair.
- Prepare your first supper at home and freeze it. Then it's just a matter of heating it up on the beach or in camp. The first dinner should be simple and easy.
- Bring a dried or canned soup for a cold day and add some fresh vegetables.
- Bring an instant meal or two. Sometimes you arrive late to your campsite or you're too tired to cook a meal.
- Bring granola bars, trail mix, cookies and other snack items.
- Some of our favourite kayak suppers are Greek salad, pasta, tacos or fajitas, hearty soups, chowders, stews and stir-fries.

FOOD STORAGE

The bottom of your kayak hold is a great place to keep food cool while paddling. When beached during the day, keep the kayak in the shade, so the food stays that way.

When bringing out food for a snack, don't leave it unattended for even a minute. Sharing with fellow campers is nice but mice, squirrels, crows, raccoons and bears would all like to share your food. Even if not normally resident, bears can swim and it's possible to find them anywhere in the Pacific Northwest. Never bring food into your tent. It's safest to store food by hanging it from a tree overnight. Use bird and squirrel-resistant container bags for hanging food (see Wildlife, page 153).

Flexible water bladders are great for packing in your kayak.

Cooking tips

- Use zip-lock bags for mixing food. For breakfast, we put an egg mixture into a bag

Food tips

and immerse it in boiling water to cook.
- Bring herbs to spice up meals and don't forget salt and pepper.
- Small, plastic roll-up cutting boards can help keep sand out of meals.
- Plan your desserts as part of the meal. Pound cakes and heavier, pre-made desserts travel well.
- Store your food in dry bags, for easy meal preparation.

Well-planned meals pay off and help you enjoy your trip.

EATING FROM THE WILD

As we strongly believe in low-impact, no-trace camping, we don't encourage harvesting food from the wild. There are just too many kayakers out there to support even a moderate amount of harvesting in popular areas. However, where stocks are high enough, some may want to indulge their hunter/gatherer instincts. Here are a few suggestions and cautions.

Fishing, crabbing and shellfish-gathering all require a licence and regulations are species specific. There are good reasons for the minimum-size and quantity restrictions, as some species and stocks are threatened and need protection.

Fishing

Use a short strong pole about 1 m (3 ft) long. You can make one by cutting down an old fishing pole. If you plan to trawl, some creative work with bungee cords and a short piece of 5-cm (2-in) plastic plumbing pipe will make a rod holder. For landing fish, you will want a small net and a club. Once the fish has been reeled in and netted, club it to death and place it under the bungees (never in the cockpit or hatches, as this may attract bears). Trawling slows a kayak considerably and there is a greater danger of capsizing when struggling with a fish or a snagged hook. A fish over 2 kg (4.4 lb) is

Paul fishing for dinner.

capable of towing a kayak. We spoke to a sport fisherman who once came to the rescue of a paddler locked in a battle worthy of Hemingway. He was many kilometres from shore and trying to land a large salmon from his kayak.

Crabbing

For crabbing, you'll need to deal with species, size and sex. There are several manufacturers of small, collapsible crab traps. You'll also need 10 to 15 m (33 to 49 ft) of light rope and a float with your name and phone number on it. The trap should have cotton thread holding part of it together; if it gets lost, the thread will rot and

release any crabs. You can use commercial bait, canned cat food (tuna flavour) or fresh clams or mussels. If using clams or mussels, crack their shells with a rock before putting them in a bait jar or bag. Pulling up the trap requires balance. Never pull the rope into the cockpit; we know of one kayaker who tried this without a PFD, tipped over, got tangled in the rope and drowned.

A collapsible crab trap is easy to transport.

Shellfish

Bivalves, such as clams, oysters and mussels, are normally harvested during months with an "r" in the name. This rules out May through August. There are two reasons for this: summer is the breeding season and quality is poor; and the likelihood of red tide and paralytic shellfish poisoning (PSP) is greater. PSP is potentially deadly.

Be aware that many commercial shellfish leases and areas with First Nations harvesting rights will be off limits. Oysters can be shucked on the beach with an oyster knife or steamed open. Yes, some people eat them raw. Shells should be returned to the water, so young oyster spat (spawn) can adhere to them. Mussels and clams are usually steamed and you should be prepared to eat some sand, unless you plan to soak them for hours (with a bit of oatmeal, some say) before cooking. Oysters and mussels are picked; clams require digging and you need to be faster at this than they are, which can be harder than it sounds.

Paralytic shellfish poisoning (PSP)

PSP is the result of algae blooms, some of which carry minute levels of toxins. These blooms are known as red tides, but not all blooms look red nor do all carry toxins. Some areas such as Barkley and Clayoquot sounds have red-tide closures 12 months of the year. The toxins concentrate in bivalves (clams, oysters, mussels, etc.) and can be deadly, if consumed by humans. Early warning signs include numbness or tingling of lips, tongue and/or fingertips, difficulty breathing, nausea, vomiting and diarrhea. The British Columbia PSP hotline for red-tide closed areas is (604) 666-2828. For Washington, it is (800) 562-5632.

Section 2
Using
Your
Kayak

6 Fitness and physical needs

WARM-UPS AND EXERCISES

Most people understand the basic concept of warming-up in anticipation of a hardy workout. An active warm-up increases blood flow and muscle temperature. Stretching encourages flexibility and an improved range of motion. Many paddlers, however, tend not to warm-up or stretch, and especially neglect the areas most prone to injury: wrists, forearms, shoulders and back.

The range of motion around joints, their connecting ligaments, tendons, muscles and bones slowly deteriorates as people age. Stiff joints and muscle tightness can begin as early as 30. Since many kayakers are in the 40 to 60 age range, improving flexibility and preparing the body for a workout is important to prevent injuries.

Joint and muscle injuries are common with kayakers. Factors such

Kayaks can take you places other boats can't go.

Fitness

as age, repetitive motion and lack of adequate conditioning can cause problems and lead to injuries. Conditioning is necessary because tendons take considerably longer to strengthen than muscles. Exercises that emphasize stretching, and weight training, help strengthen tendons and muscles.

Sometimes, in the mad rush to get into the water and begin paddling, we forget to warm-up and stretch. Try to make these activities habitual. Ideally, stretching should occur after a warm-up. The suggestions below are general; consult a physiotherapist, physician or trainer for a personalized exercise program.

Launch warm-up

Any type of aerobic activity, such as running down the beach or walking up the hill and back, will warm-up your body, as will light calisthenics, such as stepping up and down a log. Make your warm-up part of the launch. Discuss warming-up with your kayaking buddies to promote the idea. If you are fairly fit, warming-up can take as little as five minutes; otherwise, warm-up for 10.

Pre-launch stretches

Lower limb and trunk stretches can be easily accomplished on a level spot of beach or with the help of a log. Stand with one leg on a log or stump. The opposite leg has the knee slightly bent. Lower your chest toward your thigh until a stretch is felt behind the knee. Hold all stretches for 10 to 20 seconds and practice deep, rhythmic breathing. Alternate legs and stretch again.

A second standing stretch: stand on one leg with knee slightly bent, grasp the opposite ankle with your hand and pull your foot toward your behind. Repeat this exercise with your other leg and hand.

In figure 1, stand with your feet shoulder-width apart to complete a trunk stretch. With right arm above the head, slide the left hand down the leg until a stretch is felt. Alternate sides.

You may find yourself in the water, raring to go, and realize you've forgotten

STRETCHES FIG.1

to warm-up or stretch. If this occurs, begin with light paddle strokes to increase your blood flow and muscle temperature. Sprinting to the nearest island may be too quick a start and cause injury.

In-kayak stretches

Stretches can be easily accomplished during any leg of the trip. Everyone occasionally pauses on the water for a short break. There are a number of in-kayak stretches that can increase your physical comfort level.

The stretch shown in figure 2 can be done on the beach or in the kayak. Grasp the paddle and gently turn your trunk to the left and then the right. This is a good exercise for just after launching or midway in your paddle. Remember to maintain your balance or you may get more of a stretch than you were expecting.

Wrist stretches are one of the most important exercises. In figure 3, the wrist is bent back for 10 to 20 seconds and stretched with the other hand. Similarly, the wrist is bent forward in figure 4 and stretched with the opposite hand. Another exercise is to hold each wrist with the opposite hand and then rotate the held wrist in all directions. This wrist exercise is especially useful if you suffer from tendon injuries.

STRETCHES FIG.2

STRETCHES FIG.3   **STRETCHES FIG.4**

Fitness

While paddling, your hands are constantly under tension as they grip the shaft. A simple exercise is to release a finger and point it forward while continuing to paddle. This relaxes the hand muscles.

The exercise in figure 5 stretches the shoulders. Pull gently on one elbow with the opposite hand, until you feel a stretch. Alternate shoulders. Remember to stretch for 10 to 20 seconds and then repeat the exercise. Figure 6 demonstrates another shoulder stretch. In the lower position, your hand and arm are where they would be for a low brace; the upper position is similar to a high brace.

Our experiences (Paul)

I rarely see people warming-up or stretching before they set out on a kayaking trip. Gary and I are not exercise experts but we do have occasional aches and pains in our backs, shoulders, wrists and other areas. Whether we are on shore or bobbing in the kayak watching a flock of geese fly overhead, our routines are slowly changing to include "last-minute" warm-ups and stretches. We follow the old, but metrically converted, adage that a gram of prevention is worth a kilo of cure.

STRETCHES FIG.5 **STRETCHES FIG.6**

PADDLING STROKES

An efficient forward paddling stroke is key to a less tiring day of kayaking. It's easy to get into a kayak and paddle forward but it takes a few hours of practise to paddle well. A good paddling stroke combines push and pull, and is not hard to develop. The paddle should cleanly enter and exit the water and have the correct length of stroke. To an observer, a proper paddling stroke should appear fluid and effortless. One or two lessons on the beach and in the kayak, with an instructor or kayak guide, should help you acquire a basic forward paddling technique. Then, a few hours of practise on the water, concentrating on the technical aspects of the paddling stroke, will help ensure you develop a good working model.

A good paddling stroke utilizes the entire body.

Types of forward strokes
- forward paddle or touring stroke
- "box" or "rotation" power stroke

Body position, paddle length and grip
Sit upright in the kayak with your posterior firmly pressed against the seat. Place your feet or the balls of your feet on the footrests. Adjust the footrests so your knees are slightly bent and your thighs are braced under the cockpit coaming. When your feet are planted against locked footrests (with the rudder up), maximum power can be achieved. This position also allows you to control the rock of your kayak.

Fitness

Choose the right length of paddle. A short paddle might cause your hands to chafe against the gunwales of your boat; too long a paddle can be awkward. Having the right length of paddle is integral to developing a good paddling stroke.

Tables are available for choosing a paddle length based on your height, kayak width and desired angle of paddle stroke. The old method for determining your correct paddle length was to fully extend your hand above your head and then measure from this point to the ground. This method is not always accurate, though.

Common touring paddle lengths vary by 40 cm (16 in). (See Paddle length, page 37.) While there is a trend toward shorter lengths, your personal preference and experience will aid you in a decision.

Grip your paddle with hands slightly more than shoulder-width apart and equidistant from the blade ends. The grip should be relaxed and not stress the wrist or tendons. A paddle with little or no feathering (blades set to different planes) will help reduce wrist injury. If you are having or have had problems with your wrists, a smaller blade will offer less resistance to the water and, therefore, less stress on your wrists.

Performing the forward paddle or touring stroke

The forward paddle, or touring stroke, consists of both pulling and pushing the paddle. The stroke begins by reaching forward and placing the left blade, scoop (spoon side) down, on the surface of the water opposite your toes. In the same motion, twist the paddle forward and immerse the entire blade just below the surface.

Pushing stroke

At this point, your body is slightly turned to the right, away from the paddle blade in the water. As you draw the left blade back, twist your torso or upper body to the left while your right hand moves forward at or below chin level. The palm of your right hand pushes the paddle forward, parallel to the deck of the kayak. The grip of your right hand is relaxed.

PULLING STROKE

You must grip the paddle in a firm but relaxed fashion on the left (pulled) side. The paddle blade is meeting resistance as it travels through the water. On the left hand, the fingers to the first joint are perpendicular to the wrist and arm. As the arm and wrist travel backward, your grip should rotate so that your wrist does not become bent.

When practising, place your hands around a paddle shaft, look down an arm and check the alignment of your wrist and arm. The wrist and arm must be on the same plane. If the wrist is bent, it will twist and cause an injury. Any backward force should be transferred along the arm and not through a flexing wrist.

The arms and shoulders should not do all the work. The large muscles of the stomach and back are utilized when you twist your torso to the left, during the simultaneous pulling and pushing stroke.

Many novice or inexperienced paddlers rely on an abbreviated stroke. Their stroke is a shortened pull and push with no twisting of

TOURING STROKE

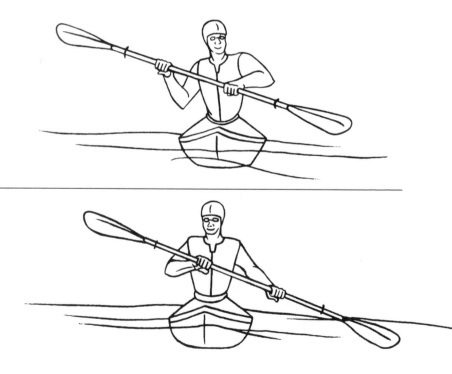

the body. If the body is twisted or rotated, the shoulders and arms work in unison with the stomach and back muscles, creating a more powerful stroke.

Your paddle exits the water opposite the hips. Past the hips, the stroke is wasted energy and may turn your boat off-course ever so slightly. Telltale signs of wasted energy are small eddies in the water.

When your left blade exits the water opposite your hips, the right hand reaches forward to plant the right paddle blade in the water near your toes. As the blade touches the water, twist it so that it smoothly cuts the surface. You are now starting the execution of the forward paddling stroke on the right side. (Some kayakers use a feathered paddle. The blade will be flicked forward by the wrist approximately 60 degrees as it contacts the surface.)

CADENCE

A good touring stroke will have a gentle and almost mechanical cadence. There is a relationship between cadence (speed of stroke) and the size of the paddle blade, the strength and stamina of the paddler and, sometimes, the prevailing sea conditions.

A person with a larger paddle blade will do fewer strokes per minute than someone with a smaller blade but each will work about as hard to go the same speed. It's a bit like two cars travelling at the same speed, with one being in second gear and the other in third.

After watching the Tour de France, it's easy to understand the meaning of cadence. Each team sets a pace that ensures that energy will be conserved for the final stages. The same principle applies to paddling.

Here are some important technical points that lend efficiency to the forward paddling stroke:

- The feet, knees and thighs are firmly placed to help deliver power to the upper body.
- The paddler's grip is relaxed, hands about a shoulder-width apart, with wrists properly positioned.
- The blade enters and exits the water cleanly. The blade enters the water near the toes and exits opposite the hip. The blade is fully submerged, just below the surface.
- During the push stroke, the hand should be at chin height or below.
- The torso should twist while pulling and pushing in order to utilize the large upper-body muscles.

Performing the "box" or "rotation" power stroke

The box or rotation paddling stroke is often used as an alternative to the touring stroke. Many paddlers combine aspects of this box stroke with the more conventional touring stroke. Although some kayakers use the box stroke as their main stroke, most use the touring stroke.

The box stroke is performed using the power of the torso, stomach and back muscles instead of the shoulder and arm muscles.

To perform a box stroke, hold your paddle roughly at chin height, with arms almost straight. This is your basic arm posture for the

BOX POWER STROKE

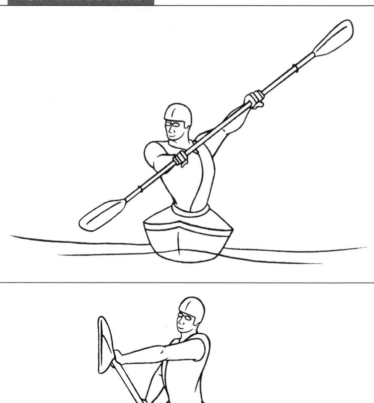

stroke. Rotate your body about 45 degrees to the right and place the left blade into the water near your toes. The paddle will enter the water more vertically than with the touring stroke. Your left arm is straight and locked; your right or upper arm is slightly bent. The key is to rotate your body to the left approximately 90 degrees so that it ends up 45 degrees to the line of the kayak. At the end of the stroke, your right arm will be straight and your left arm slightly bent. This leaves you in position to start your stroke on the right. Adding a sweeping motion away from the kayak will give extra power. This torso/shoulder rotation is a powerful type of stroke.

The transition of the paddle stroke from the left to right side (or side to side) looks like a movement through a figure 8. At the end of the stroke (left side), your left hand is approximately at hip height, your right hand at head height, and the angle of the paddle is approximately 30 degrees from vertical. If you watch your hands executing the left and right strokes, you can easily visualize a figure 8 in front of you.

It is easy to feel and see the difference between a basic forward paddling stroke utilizing the arms and shoulders and one utilizing a combination of arms, shoulders, torso, stomach and back muscles. The torso/shoulder rotation, whether used in the box stroke or the touring stroke, will help you become a more efficient paddler.

Our experiences (Paul)

We've paddled with kayakers who were using too short a stroke, had a poor entry into the water or were just using their arms to power along. Not only did their paddling lack smoothness and fluidity, they were working harder than we were and going slower. Paddling should resemble the graceful motion of tai chi. Once you have learned the proper techniques, they help you save energy, stay relaxed and keep pace with your buddies. All in all, a good paddling stroke is like an art form: it needs to be practised with an eye for technique and fluidity.

Although we mainly use the forward touring stroke, Gary and I change to the box stroke, routinely, during our trips to give arm, shoulder, back and stomach muscles a change of pace. We will also change to the box stroke for extra speed, when needed. The large muscles in your upper body eventually tire when using the same method repeatedly. A little variety spices up your paddling day.

BALANCING AND BRACING

Anyone who has used a walking stick over rough terrain knows that being able to extend an artificial limb will aid balance. Your paddle is much like a walking stick. It can stabilize you for support or can be used to slap the water in order to prevent capsizing.

Many beginning kayakers will sit and wait for an oncoming large wave, whether from a boat's wake or weather generated. However, if you are actively paddling, you will be more stable than you would be if sitting stationary. This is similar to the difference in being on a moving bicycle and on an almost stationary one.

Staying upright in your kayak is a piece of cake when water conditions are not rough. When conditions worsen, though, balance becomes more important and bracing may be needed. Bracing is mainly used to recover balance, by slapping the water, or to prepare to be hit by a breaking wave.

Balance

When it comes to balance, you need to use your head. If you can keep your head directly above your boat, balancing is easy. The head, a mass of bone, raises the centre of gravity. If the head tips to left or right, the balance of the boat can change quickly.

So how do you keep your head in the right place when you and your boat start to tip? If your paddle is in the air on the side you are leaning toward, you can slap the water with it. A better method, though, is to bend at the hip so that only the kayak and the lower half of your body are tipping. To be able to make either of these moves effectively, you need to "wear" the boat. This means having proper padding, so that your thighs are tight against the hull and deck, and proper footrests, so you won't slide in your seat.

Some of us have better balance than others. As we age, however, balance worsens and reflexes slow. Fortunately, we can improve our balance and sharpen our reflexes by practising a few simple exercises, which are described in the rest of this chapter. For those who want more information on the subject, we recommend *The Bombproof Roll and Beyond*, by Paul Dutky.

Warm water and air temperatures are preferable when practising, as you will most likely get wet. We use a local lake in the summer and rent an indoor swimming pool during the winter. If you get six or more people together, renting a pool can be quite affordable. We

Swimming pools are good for practising your techniques.

pair up and take turns practising our techniques; when one person practises, the other spots for safety. Make sure participants stay safely away from hard objects such as the edge of the pool (unless using it for the exercise).

Balance exercise 1: Sit in your kayak in calm water, slowly raise a knee and bend at the hips, so the kayak is at an angle. Keep your head directly over the kayak. See how far you can tilt the boat and still feel comfortable. Use your paddle for balance by having a blade flat on the surface of the water. Repeat this procedure, using the other knee and tilting in the other direction. Do this exercise again, while holding on to the edge of the pool, another kayak or someone standing in the water.

Balance exercise 2: Tilt your kayak as in exercise 1 and paddle a short distance but only on one side (the side the boat is leaning toward). Repeat the exercise tilted the other way, paddling only on that side.

Balance exercise 3: This is more difficult. Tilt the kayak and paddle normally (on both sides). Tilt in the other direction and try again.

Types of bracing
- slap recovery support
- low brace
- high brace

Slap recovery support

The slap brace is mainly used when you lose your balance. By slapping the face (or back) of your paddle on the water you can recover your balance. This method works well if your paddle is in the air at the right moment. If your paddle is in the water on the side you are tipping toward, you won't have time for a slap but you still can get some support from flattening the blade (parallel to the water surface) and pushing down with a jerk. Paddle slaps can be combined with a forward paddle stroke to add to your recovery. (The face of the blade is the surface that faces the paddler during a normal forward paddle stroke. The face often has the brand name written on it.)

Slap support exercise 1: Tilt your kayak to the point where it will tip over, and recover by slapping the water with the paddle face. Try it again using the back of the paddle blade. Try this while tilting toward the other side.

Slap support exercise 2: Try a tilt and recover your balance using a slap combined with a forward stroke. Be careful not to extend your arm too far, to avoid a pulled muscle or other injury.

SLAP RECOVERY

Slap support exercise 3: Do a tilt with the paddle in the water on the side you are tilting toward and recover by either pushing down with the paddle or by a combination of pushing down and stroking forward.

Low brace

The low brace is used when you are broached (hit on the side) by a small breaking wave. Small, in this case, means not much higher than the deck of your kayak. If the wave is hitting your left side, extend your paddle (blade face up) out to the left and lean on the paddle shaft, into the wave. The force of the wave will knock you to the right, so leaning to the left needs to be timed correctly.

During a low brace, the paddle shaft should be held parallel to the water surface and at the height of the breaking wave. Your elbows should be extended to the sides and the hand closest to the wave stretched slightly out. The hand on your other side should be above the corresponding thigh. Your elbows should be higher than your hands and you should look as if you're pushing down with your wrists.

You need small breaking waves to practise low bracing and this will most likely require a West Coast beach and shallow water. Practise with an empty kayak, not a loaded one. This type of practice may cause injury, as tipping over in shallow water can result in some hard bumps against the ocean floor.

LOW BRACE

High brace

The high brace is used when larger breaking waves broach your kayak. These waves may be at shoulder height. Hold your paddle with the blade face down and the paddle shaft parallel to the water surface. Elbows are extended out to the side and your hands should be higher than your elbows. The wave-side blade is even with the top of the breaking wave, and that arm is extended out slightly. The other hand (away from the wave) is held close to the corresponding shoulder. As in the low brace, lean into the wave at the right moment.

We hope that you will never be in the position of needing a high brace. By taking these breaking waves bow-on, instead of sideways, you should be able to paddle through them.

HIGH BRACE

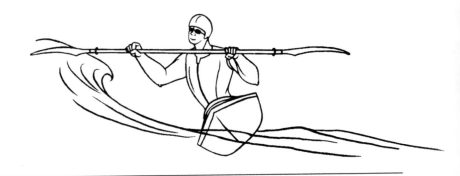

Edging and leaning

Edging and leaning are used for turning and can be a lot of fun. Edging is a bit like an ice skater doing a quick stop and sending ice flying, while leaning resembles a bicyclist rounding a sharp corner. Practicing edging and leaning is a good way to reinforce skills.

For quick turns, you normally use the paddle to create drag. By tilting your boat, leaning and dragging the paddle, you will be able to perform sharper turns. Some kayak designs (usually with hard chines) will turn by tilting alone and do not require dragging the paddle. These boats often turn in the opposite direction than the tilt.

By moving your head and shoulder over the water and leaning onto your paddle for support, you can use your kayak's speed to

Fitness

turn. This is all done in one motion. If you execute this very well, it's possible to touch the water with your armpit and immerse part of the sprayskirt. Even when not done to this extreme, leaning is a very effective turning manoeuvre.

Leaning exercise 1: Tilt the boat, as in balance exercise 1, but do this while moving at a good rate of speed. See if the boat turns and in which direction. Repeat, only this time drag a paddle in the water to assist your turn.

Balance exercises will increase your comfort level.

Edging exercise 1: While moving fairly fast in the water, extend your paddle in the low-brace position and lean over to tilt your

LEANING

EDGING AND TURNING

Paddles can be used as brakes and rudders.

kayak. Before you come to a stop, push down on your paddle, as discussed in slap support exercise 3, end your lean and return to an upright position. The angle of your paddle blade and how your arms are held are very important. The back of the blade must be at a slight angle to the surface of the water to give uplift as it skims across the surface. If you are leaning to the right, your left hand should be holding the paddle shaft so that it almost touches the cockpit coaming. Your right hand should be extended a little way out and slightly aft. This exercise takes practice to perfect.

Our experiences (Gary)

We make practising these exercises a family activity at least once or twice a year. There are always a few newbies with us, trying the exercises for the first time. Usually, they are either afraid to try tilting very far or they get really carried away and are soon doing a wet-exit. Practice builds confidence and improves both balance and reflexes. When you think about it, a reflex is really a subconscious reaction that happens in a split second. Your subconscious won't kick in appropriately unless your conscious mind has had lots of experience in similar situations.

7 Kayak safety

BASIC SAFETY FOR KAYAKING

We cannot overemphasize the importance of safety. Every year, kayakers get into trouble and, often, it's the most experienced ones who push the envelope just a little too far. Most get out of trouble, but each year, a few die. Usually, kayakers die because safety was ignored.

Beginning kayakers who think they can go anywhere, in any kinds of conditions, with their magical craft are also likely to get into trouble. Kayaks are stable and, in the right hands, can travel in pretty extreme conditions. They can also turn over in the blink of an eye, as a result of some small error in judgment. Getting back in may not be as simple as it was during the pool practice session.

Ideally, beginning kayakers should start by paddling with experienced kayakers. Join a paddling club or take some guided trips, if you are unable to find a seasoned or experienced partner.

It's safer to paddle in groups.

Safety on the water involves knowing and interpreting marine conditions. Kayakers should also carry basic safety equipment, paddle with a partner, and know self-rescue and assisted-rescue techniques. Having said that, however, kayaking is still a safe watersport. What follows are some basic safety guidelines:

- Check the marine conditions for your area by listening to a marine radio forecast, phoning the local marine weather office or checking www.weatheroffice.ec.gc.ca/marine/region_03_e.html (or through the Reference section at www.easykayaker.com). Remember that winds vary considerably, depending on the geology and hydrology of the local area. The marine weather radio forecast (Coast Guard) gives wind and sea conditions for specific sites. Usually, these sites are points and lighthouse stations that are more exposed than paddling areas tend to be. Wind and sea conditions in coves, bays and inlets are usually slightly more favourable than at the weather reference site but this is not always the case.

- Know the tides. Many marine-related stores offer free tide guides. An official tide and current table from Fisheries and Oceans Canada can be purchased from most marine suppliers for about

$8. Volume 5 covers southern Vancouver Island, Georgia Strait and Puget Sound. Volume 6 covers western and northern Vancouver Island and the adjacent mainland coast. Volume 7 covers the northern BC coast and Queen Charlotte Islands. The Canadian Hydrographic Service tides and currents site at Fisheries and Oceans Canada (www.lau.chs-shc.dfo-mpo.gc.ca) is a great resource for paddlers. You can print out tide tables for the exact area and date you want. The National Oceanic and Atmospheric Administration's (NOAA's) National Ocean Service provides a similar resource at tides-online.noaa.gov. Tides may determine your launch site and destination. They also cause currents. Check the flood and ebb for the area where you are planning on paddling.

- Have the proper marine chart for the area you will be paddling and carry a compass. Charts indicate current flows of one knot or stronger for most navigable waters. You can travel at about 3 to 4

Planning the perfect trip.

knots (5.5 to 7.5 km/h) in your kayak but paddling against a three-knot current is no fun. Charts are available from most marine supply stores. A compass can be important in fog or darkness (see Compasses, page 132). Having a GPS (see GPS, page 138) is beneficial, but you should still have a compass.

- Compare wind direction and tidal flow. If tide and wind are moving in the same direction, water conditions are often fairly calm. When the wind is pushing against the tidal current, waves are created.

- Attach the paddle to your kayak with a paddle leash. If you do go over, you won't have to worry about losing your paddle and can concentrate on grabbing the boat. If you're kayaking alone (not recommended) and you capsize, you'll need your paddle to perform a self-rescue. (People proficient at the Eskimo roll do not normally use a paddle leash.)

- Take a minimum of 1 L (34 fl oz) of water, or 3 L (102 fl oz) on hot days, for a day's kayaking. Have the water accessible while paddling. It's easy to get dehydrated, which can cause headaches, low energy or worse problems. Having a snack will help maintain energy levels.

- Have at least the basic safety equipment required by Coast Guard regulations plus a paddle float and one spare paddle per group. A small first-aid kit, toilet paper and warm extra clothes are also recommended.

- Stay with your group. Always kayak with at least one other person and stay within calling or whistle-blowing distance. An assisted rescue is much easier than a self-rescue. Lone kayaks are hard for other boaters to see. By staying in a group, you are less likely to risk a collision and large boats have a better chance of seeing a group of kayaks on their radar. There are rules of the road, or collision regulations (www.ccg-gcc.gc.ca/obs-bsn/main_e.htm), that are the marine equivalents of driving laws and govern who has the right of way in any situation.

- Know how to perform a self-rescue and an assisted rescue. You should know how to wet-exit from your kayak, in case you capsize, and how to use a paddle float to do a self-rescue and wet-entry. Wet-exiting is scary, for most people, but it's really very easy. We strongly recommend that you learn basic rescue techniques and then practise them yearly with a partner, in the warm waters of a lake or pool. Do not expect to be able to do an Eskimo roll, as this is an advanced technique; however, learning to brace with your paddle is not difficult and well worth practising.

- File a float plan. Let someone know where you're going paddling and approximately when you will return.

Coastal regulations for kayaking

Safe boating regulations for kayaks under and over 6 m (19.5 ft) in length can be found at www.ccg-gcc.gc.ca/obs-bsn/equipment_e.htm, under "Canoes, kayaks, rowboats and rowing shells not over 6 m in length." For your convenience, the information for kayaks under 6 m (19.5 ft) is included below:

- one Canadian-approved personal flotation device (PFD) or lifejacket of appropriate size for each person on board
- one buoyant heaving line of not less than 15 m (50 ft) in length
- one manual propelling device (paddle) or an anchor with not less than 15 m (50 ft) of cable, rope or chain in any combination
- one bailer or manual water pump fitted with or accompanied by sufficient hose to enable a person to pump over the vessel's side

Kayak safety

- one sound-signalling device or appliance (usually a whistle attached to your lifejacket or an air horn)
- navigation lights that meet applicable standards if the craft is to be operated after sunset, before sunrise or in periods of restricted visibility

Many double kayaks are over 6 m (19.5 ft) in length and require the above equipment, plus flares. Kayaks should also be equipped with paddle floats, for self-rescue. Regulations for Washington State can be found online at www.boatwashington.org/minimum_ equipment_requirements.htm.

Hypothermia

Hypothermia, or abnormally low body temperature, is probably the main cause of death in sea kayaking. There are two main types of hypothermia: steady heat loss through slow exposure to cold and quick heat loss through immersion in cold water. If the air temperature is cold or the paddler is already feeling cold, hypothermia can occur in as little as 10 minutes in BC's coastal waters. If a person stays quiet, death will probably occur after about two and a half to three hours. If you burn up precious energy swimming for shore or attempting multiple wet-entries, death can come much sooner.

If you are going paddling in cold waters, you need to be prepared for possible immersion. For cool or cold weather paddling, taking along a change of clothes in a dry bag is a must. Hot drinks in a thermos, fire starter and a sleeping bag or space blanket are also recommended. Dressing for a cold ocean dip is a smart choice. A neoprene wetsuit or a drysuit provides the most effective defence against cold water.

Advanced hypothermia must be treated quickly. If the kayaker is unconscious or displays the "umbles"—stumbles, fumbles, grumbles, mumbles—this demonstrates changes in motor coordination. If medical help is not nearby, immediate steps must be taken, such as: find shelter, remove victim's wet clothing and replace with dry clothing, start a fire, get victim to drink hot fluids, eat food such as trail mix and increase physical activity. Avoid alcohol, coffee and tobacco. Warm victim, in a sleeping bag, with your body heat.

Common sense helps prevent hypothermia. Recognize the conditions that may cause it and take the necessary steps to avoid it.

RESCUE TECHNIQUES

If you venture away from shore, you'd better know how to get back into your kayak from the water. No matter what size boat you're in, capsizing is always a possibility. Getting out of a kayak after capsizing is called a "wet-exit." Getting back in from the water is called a "wet-entry." Learning the wet-exit is straightforward; all you need to know is how to release your sprayskirt if it doesn't self-release, and to stay with the boat. Your legs virtually fall out of the kayak once it's upside down.

A wet-entry, on the other hand, is not easy, unless you have practised the techniques. If seas are rough, it may not be easy even for the experienced. You won't have the opportunity to choose the spot for your accidental capsize but you can choose where not to capsize by not paddling there. When conditions are rough, try to paddle along beaches and easy-to-land shorelines and keep your route away from the rocks. Gary has twice, had to deal with a novice paddler wet-exiting; both times he'd kept the paddling route to a safe area where he could pull the wet kayaker to shore quickly instead of bothering with a wet-entry. It would be a nightmare to try to rescue an inexperienced paddler being pounded into the rocks by the surf.

There are two main types of rescues: self-rescue and assisted rescue. The assisted rescue is the easiest and the preferred method, as long as the person in the water doesn't do something stupid and put you both in the water. Don't go kayaking without learning these techniques, either from a kayaking course or an experienced paddler. We spoke to one beginner who went kayaking off the West Coast of Vancouver Island by himself and capsized. The current carried him away from the beach and he spent 40 minutes trying to do a wet-entry (he didn't know how). A powerboat rescued him.

Let's start with the **self-rescue** technique. Your first requirement is to paddle without much on the deck of the kayak that will get in the way of a rescue. Once you have capsized, you must right the kayak, and in doing so, try to remove as much water as possible. At the same time, don't lose your paddle (a paddle leash is recommended).

Attach your paddle float to the blade of the paddle, slide the other blade onto the kayak under the shock cords behind the cockpit. You now have an outrigger for stabilization (see drawings). Next, with your head pointed toward the rudder, place one hand on the paddle shaft and the other hand on the far side of the cockpit coaming, and

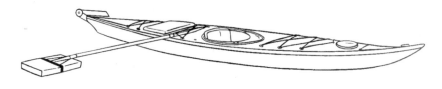

SELF RESCUE

crawl up so that your chest comes onto the rear deck. Swing your legs into the cockpit. You will now be partly in the cockpit and staring at the rudder, with the paddle blade under your chest or stomach. While leaning slightly on the paddle shaft, rotate your body so you're right side up and finish sliding into the cockpit. Now you need to get the rest of the water out of your kayak, retrieve your paddle from behind you and detach the paddle float. And you get to do this in waves how high? It's fairly simple to do a self-rescue in a swimming pool. Real-life conditions can be something else. One last note: for some of us, crawling up onto the back deck isn't easy with a PFD on. One solution is to carry a 3-m (10-ft) rope tied into a loop. Slip this loop over the cockpit lip or coaming and let it extend into the water as a stirrup. This makes climbing back in much easier.

The **assisted rescue** starts out the same way. Instead of using a paddle float as an outrigger, you will have your boat steadied by another kayaker who is still dry and afloat. If you are in the water, the first step is to right your boat and position it in a **T-formation** with the assisting kayak, so that your bow is even with your rescuer's lap. Push down on the rudder area while your rescuer lifts the bow onto his or her lap. At this point, you both turn the kayak upside down to empty the water from the cockpit (see drawing). This is not a manoeuvre to try with a fully loaded kayak or in rough sea

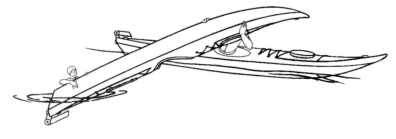

ASSISTED RESCUE

conditions. If the T-formation isn't possible, proceed as described below and then pump out the water after you have completed the wet-entry.

After the kayak is righted and slid off the rescuer's lap, it is positioned alongside the assisting kayak but facing the opposite direction. Now, you have two kayaks side by side. The rescuer reaches over with both hands and grabs both sides of the cockpit coaming a little forward of the centre of the cockpit opening. This makes both boats very stable. The capsized kayaker can then crawl up on the rear deck, as if performing a self-rescue (but without the outrigger), slide into the cockpit and swivel around. In a variation of this technique, the capsized kayaker enters from the opposite side by crawling over the rescuer's boat to get into his or her own boat.

Once you have learned these rescue techniques, practise them. It's hard on your chest and stomach, and it scratches boats, but it can be lifesaving. If possible, find a beach on a warm sunny day, with some wave action, and try the techniques.

It's good to practise your rescue techniques with your paddling buddies.

EQUIPMENT FOR A KAYAK DAY TRIP

Day trips are more enjoyable if well-planned. Some of the following items are overkill for a two-hour summer paddle but make sense if you are going out for a six-hour jaunt in January:

- Equipment: In a kayak under 6 m (19.5 ft) in length, the basics for a day's paddle include a PFD, sprayskirt, pump or bailer, sponge, paddle, whistle, paddle float, spare paddle (one per group) and a 15-m (50-ft) buoyant heaving line.

- Navigation: Take a compass, charts for the area (in a waterproof case, if the charts aren't laminated), and tide and current tables. Optional is a GPS unit (great in the fog), if you know how to use one.

- Safety: Include a towline (unless the buoyant heaving line is suitable for towing), duct tape, first-aid kit, foil survival blanket, waterproof matches and kayak repair kit. For summertime day trips, the kayak repair kit can consist of a partial roll of duct tape. You may want to include flares and a weather or VHF radio. If you get into trouble, a VHF radio is often a lifesaver. It will connect you to other nearby boats and to the Coast Guard.

First aid kit and survival kit.

- Gear: Rain gear (preferably light) or paddling jacket, cap or sun hat, paddling boots (wetsuit booties) or good sandals, quick-drying shorts, sunscreen, sunglasses, flashlight and extra batteries (if paddling in the evening), toilet paper, water bottles (up to 3 L or 102 fl oz of water per day) and paddling gloves are all extras that you may want along. During the cool part of the year, a change of warm clothes and long underwear (preferably polypropylene) or a wetsuit are advised.

- Additional optional items: crab trap, knife, food, fire starter, fishing gear and licence, camera, binoculars and cell phone. Use common sense; don't drag out more gear than necessary for your trip but be prepared if you plan to paddle in an isolated area.

Kayak repair kit

A kayak repair kit or emergency repair kit is an important part of your equipment. At least one person in your group should carry a kit for on-the-spot repair. The repair kit may be kept in zip-lock bags and stored in a dry bag or kept in a waterproof container. Its make-up will depend on the type of paddling you plan to do, the materials your kayaks are made of and how far away help will be. These are some items to pack in a repair kit:

- roll of good-quality duct tape
- waterproof tape, such as Denso, for quick repairs on wet surfaces
- hand towel to dry repair area
- additional heavy-duty zip-lock bags
- length of rudder cable with cable crimps
- spare nuts and bolts for your rudder and pedals
- pliers and screw driver, or Leatherman tool, stored in zip-lock bags
- length of cord to replace lines or bungee cords
- extra hatch and bungee-cord clips
- small tube of marine silicone caulking or adhesive for sealing holes and leaks in bulkheads
- small washers for sealing holes
- neoprene patches and neoprene contact cement
- waterproof matches, lighter and candle
- sewing needle and nylon thread

MARINE WINDS AND WEATHER

A typical day trip should begin by checking the marine weather forecast for the area you will be paddling and observing such obvious conditions as cloud cover and wind level. The marine broadcast should indicate the wind levels for your chosen kayaking area. Winds are generally predictable and conform to regular patterns, with a few exceptions. Local knowledge can help with these exceptions. Talk to local kayakers and other boaters if the paddling area is new to you.

The Coast Guard and Environment Canada provide around-the-clock marine forecasts. They can be heard over VHF and weather radios. Weather Radio Canada (Environment Canada) broadcasts at frequencies from 162.40 to 162.55 MHz and the Coast Guard broadcasts at 161.65 MHz. Marine forecasts can also be found at

Easykayaking Basics

www.weatheroffice.ec.gc.ca/forecast/canada/bc_e.html. Environment Canada has a weather information phone line at 1-900-565-1111. The forecasts are synopses of weather conditions that will most likely influence local waters. Knowledge of technical or common terms used on the broadcasts can be helpful. Wind orientation is the direction the wind is coming from; in other words, a southeast wind is blowing from southeast to northwest. Wind speed is measured in knots. A knot is one nautical mile per hour (1.85 km/h).

Light winds:	0 - 10 knots (0 - 19 km/h)
Moderate:	11 - 19 knots (20 - 36 km/h)
Strong (small-craft warning):	20 - 33 knots (37 - 61 km/h)
Gale warning:	34 - 47 knots (62 - 87 km/h)
Storm warning:	48 - 63 knots (88 - 117 km/h)
Hurricane warning:	64 knots or more (118+ km/h)

The most frequent warnings on the marine broadcasts are "small-craft warnings." This means that a strong wind is expected. "Gale-force" winds are next in strength and even stronger are "storm-force" winds. Wave heights are represented in metres. On the West Coast, swell heights are sometimes given and then wind-wave heights or combined swell-and-wind-wave heights.

Weather reports often speak about "highs" and "lows." The net difference between a high and a low is called a pressure gradient. Winds travel from a high to a low and are affected by the earth as it spins (the Coriolis force). This force deflects the winds to the right, in the northern hemisphere. There are many factors, from centrifugal force to friction, that influence how winds travel.

The weather can change quickly on the West Coast.

When you're planning a paddle, familiarity with local sea and land breezes will be helpful. It's quite possible that the area you are headed for will be protected from mainstream winds but exposed to local ones.

Sea breezes occur when bodies of land and water heat up and cool down at different rates. Sea breezes most often happen on warm sunny days during the spring and summer, when the temperature of the land is typically higher than that of the ocean. In the morning, land and water start out at similar temperatures. As the sun beats down, the land heats quickly while the ocean, which can absorb a lot of heat without warming, stays at a more constant temperature. Once a significant temperature differential exists, a sea breeze begins blowing onto shore.

Land breezes are common in fall and winter and begin with the cooling of low-lying air. On a calm evening, a temperature differential can occur between nearby land and water masses, causing a cool wind to blow offshore. This wind is called a "land breeze." A land breeze is stronger closer to the coastline.

Every paddler has a comfort level. That level often changes as experience grows. After paddling heavy seas, a person realizes that kayaks are incredibly stable watercraft. When you see beginners white-knuckled in a little chop, it's because they have exceeded their comfort level. Even for those of us with higher comfort levels, paddling in rough water is generally not as enjoyable as kayaking in benign conditions, where you can relax and focus your attention on the scenery.

We have often gone paddling when the marine forecast has predicted a small-craft warning, using our local knowledge to choose a more protected spot. We don't advise paddlers to take chances, however. If strong winds are predicted or weather conditions look unstable, we usually eliminate open crossings from our route. We also consider wind direction and avoid areas with large open bodies of water, where waves can build in height. We have paddled many times in winds that will blow the hat off your head, but because there was no large expanse of water to our windward side, the waves were tiny.

The Pacific Northwest offers a huge variety of paddling destinations, both sheltered and open, and there is usually somewhere not too far away where you can paddle without exceeding your comfort level. An added benefit to developing experience as a kayaker is that you will become much more attuned to winds, weather, tides and currents.

Kayak safety

MARINE RADIOS

Communication and safety are the primary reasons for making a VHF (very high frequency) marine radio part of your kayaking equipment. You can call for help, set up a rendezvous or listen to the marine weather forecast. Listening to a VHF radio can be entertaining and you can sometimes glean important information, such as when a large ferry announces that it is about to enter the same narrow waterway you are paddling. You might hear where the fish are biting and if whales have been spotted.

VHF radios aren't cheap. You are not required to have a licence in order to operate one but you must have an operator's certificate. You need to understand radio lingo and which channels to use or avoid. For many kayakers, this is a new realm.

What is a VHF marine radio?

A VHF radio is much like a CB radio but its use is exclusive to the marine environment. These radios allow two-way conversations. VHF radios are available in portable, hand-held models and stationary models. For the purpose of kayaking, the portable, hand-held type is the practical choice.

Purchasing a VHF radio

VHF radios are available at most marine supply stores and many coastal outdoor-recreation outlets. Radio manufacturers have web sites that list available features and specifications. These are some things to consider:

- features (number of channels, scanning, etc)
- ease of use
- output power
- whether the unit is waterproof and to what depth
- size and weight
- battery type and length of operating time per charge
- price and warranty

Features to look for include the number of channels and weather channels (WX), plus scanning and programmable priority scanning options. Often, you will want to monitor more than one channel. Priority scanning allows you to select a priority channel. When in scanning mode, that channel will be given priority over any other channels you've programmed for scanning. Some radios have an automatic weather alert.

Ease of use refers to the readability of the display, the number and functions of the keys (buttons) and whether or not they are backlit for night use. Specific keys for channels 16/9 and weather channels are very useful. Most units will have these, plus an up-and-down key for going through the channels. There are also keys for scanning, programming, transmitting, setting the output power and turning on a light.

The display should tell you more than what channel you are on. It should also show any restricted use for that channel for your country of operation, your transmit power setting and other information. The volume and squelch switches should be easy to adjust.

Some units are waterproof but many of these are only rated to a 1-m (3-ft) depth for 30 minutes. Most don't float. Having a waterproof model means that you can carry it in your PFD and not worry if it gets wet while you're paddling in the rain. Waterproof, form-fitting pouches are available for VHF radios but these can be a bit cumbersome. Buoyancy can be added to the pouch with a neoprene jacket.

If possible, have the VHF radio attached to you, instead of to your boat. Should you capsize in the wind and let go of your kayak, it is almost impossible to swim after it, since your PFD will slow you down. You won't be able to call for help unless the radio is with you. Of course, the radio should be small and light enough to be attached to the PFD or fit in one of its pockets.

An important feature is whether the unit comes with rechargeable batteries and has an adequate battery life. Check the unit's specifications for predicted battery life. Some models come with both rechargeable batteries and a holder for disposable batteries. Unless one charge can last the length of your trip, using disposable batteries makes sense. It's wise to choose a VHF radio with a battery indicator as part of its display.

VHF hand-held radios cost from $150 to $400. Waterproof models are at the higher end of this range. Three popular brands are Horizon (from Yaesu, www.yaesu.com), Icon (www.icon.co.jp/world/index.html) and Uniden (www.uniden.com). As with any purchase, price and warranty are important but these should not be the primary factors in choosing a radio. A VHF radio may save your life or someone else's. What is that worth?

Obtaining a restricted operator's certificate

Radio airwaves are governed by Industry Canada in Canada and by the Federal Communications Commission in the US. By law, anyone operating a VHF radio over Canadian waters must have a radio telephone operator's restricted (maritime) certificate. Kayakers and other small pleasure boaters are exempt from this requirement in the US.

The certificate requires passing a test. You can take a course through a local chapter of the Canadian Power & Sail Squadrons or on-line at www.cps-ecp.org.

Once you obtain a certificate, it's good for life and recognized internationally. You are not required to carry your certificate when operating your radio and you do not need a certificate to purchase a VHF radio; in reality, many radio owners do not have certificates.

Using a VHF radio

There is a protocol for using a VHF radio. The radio can only be used on land, if calling someone on the water. Each marine channel is assigned a purpose. Channel 16 is the Hail and Distress channel and is supposed to be monitored by all boaters equipped with a radio. It is monitored 24/7 by the Coast Guard. As long as it isn't being used for an emergency, you can call (hail) another boater on channel 16. Channel 9 is also used as a hailing channel.

The calling procedure is to listen to make sure the channel is clear, then state the name of the boat you are calling three times, followed by the name of your kayak. As most kayaks aren't named, you may have to get creative to meet this part of the requirements. If your call is not answered, you must wait three minutes before trying again. Once you make contact with the other boat, you must change to a working channel. Calls on channel 16 should not exceed 30 seconds.

You can find a list of working channels open to pleasure-boat use in your VHF user's guide or on-line. Channel 6 is for ship-to-ship safety messages and for searches (including aircrafts). Many communities and certain industries have favourite channels. The whale-watching tour companies in Victoria use a common channel. Clayoquot fish farms use channels 8, 10 and 80. The community of Ahousat uses channel 68, Hot Springs Cove uses 66 and Kyuquot uses 14. The VHF is a lifeline for coastal villages; most homes, businesses, cars and boats have radios.

When placing a distress call, "mayday" is used when someone's life is threatened and "pan-pan" when someone is in trouble that is not life threatening. A boat that has lost its steering or power would use "pan-pan." The standard procedure is to use channel 16, say "mayday" or "pan-pan" three times and then give your boat's name. Then repeat "mayday" or "pan-pan" once and your boat's name. After that, give your location (using local landmarks, compass directions, and longitude and latitude, if possible). Then state the nature of your distress and the kind of assistance needed. You will also need to describe your boat as a kayak and include its colour and the number of people involved.

On any call, use the term "over" to signify that you want a reply and the term "clear" or "out" to signify that your conversation is finished. Do not use CB lingo like "breaker-breaker" or police codes like "10-4." Always speak slowly and don't shout into the radio. Never cut into someone else's conversation.

Hand-held VHF radios have a fairly weak transmitting power (five watts or less) compared to stationary VHF radios (typically 25 watts). Often you can hear people who won't be able to hear you. Hills, trees and other obstructions easily block the signal, which has a short range even for stationary units. If you aren't able to reach the other party, paddle to a different location and try again. You may have to rely on a nearby boat or other stationary VHF user to relay your

File a float plan before heading out.

Kayak safety

message. This is true of remote locations like Nuchatlitz, even when calling for a water taxi.

Despite the weak transmitting power of hand-held VHF radios, they may still be too strong for harbour areas. Most radios have a switch to limit power to one watt, for use in these locations.

The bottom line when using a VHF radio is to:
- comply with the standards for maritime radio telephones
- use the proper frequencies
- use standard expressions and protocol
- comply with priorities
- keep conversations to the point, avoiding unnecessary chatter
- refrain from using offensive language

Our experiences (Gary)

Although the VHF radio course will take time and money, we highly recommend it. The course teaches the proper usage of all the specific radio terms, such as "go ahead," "say again" and "seelonce." Although we've heard most of these terms before, we may not be fluent in using them. For instance, do you know the difference between "affirmative" and "roger"? ("Roger" means that you received the message; "affirmative" means you agree with the message.)

Paul and I each carry a VHF radio in our PFD and can monitor weather and large boat traffic or call a water taxi, if bad weather pins us down. A radio is also useful when we split our paddling group and want to meet later. Even though we may be well into the wilderness, there are always boats in the area; being able to call for help in an emergency provides peace of mind.

FILING A FLOAT PLAN

Whether you're heading off for a day paddle or an extended trip, you should always file a float plan. The plan might be as simple as letting someone know where you're launching, who you're paddling with, your proposed route and when you plan to return. The idea is for someone to know when to call out a search party and where that party should search. With any luck, you will never be the subject of a search party, but it pays to be safe.

8 Kayak navigation

HOW TO NAVIGATE WITH A COMPASS

Why should you have a compass? An obvious reason is fog but that's not the only reason. On more than one trip, we have ended up crossing into the sunset. (Sounds a bit like the end of a cowboy movie.) We are usually returning home and squeezing in as much paddling as possible on our last day out. Paddling into the sunset may sound romantic but can be blinding. It's often difficult to see the distant shore, even when it's fairly close. That's another good reason for a compass.

Sometimes we paddle after sunset. Although the light lingers in the evening during most of the summer, the shoreline loses definition and distant landmarks aren't recognizable. Taking a compass bearing should keep you headed in the right direction.

Rafting together is a good time to look at a chart.

Navigation

A compass can also be used by a group of paddlers to decide on a specific direction or bearing. We'll sometimes gather our kayaks and decide what to aim for on the far shore. Barring fog, blinding sun or darkness, we can usually see the far shore but the landmark we choose may not be easily distinguishable from other, similar shoreline features. So we will say, for example, "Let's head toward that brown patch at about 275 degrees." Now everyone using a compass will know which of the three brown patches we mean.

Is a compass still needed if you have a GPS? Most definitely. A GPS doesn't work like a compass. It won't give you an accurate direction unless you are moving fairly fast, at about 2 knots (3 km/h) or more. It won't operate without batteries, or in the shadow of mountains and cliffs, and most units don't work when wet. Some kayakers suggest having two compasses along because our subconscious won't trust just one. Have you ever thought, "This compass can't be right; there must be something wrong with it"?

One problem with a compass, that doesn't bother a GPS unit, is drift. You can take an accurate compass bearing but wind or current, or a combination of the two, can easily push you off course. Even on a visual crossing, your heading should always take drift into consideration.

Types of compasses

Kayak compasses generally fall into three categories: hand-held, strap-on and mounted. A small, hand-held compass can be handy for hiking, cross-country skiing or snowshoeing, or even for locating a star. A larger compass mounted on the deck of your kayak will have better graduations, for more accurate readings. Compasses are balanced for a latitude zone (inclination) but specialized "global" compasses are designed for any magnetic zone, with the needle and magnet as separate units. For most non-globetrotting paddlers, this feature may be superfluous. The main considerations when buying a compass are price, accuracy, type (mounted, strap-on or hand-held), quality, durability and special features.

Most paddlers like a strap-on or mounted compass. A strap-on compass can be attached to your bungee cords quickly and easily. There are advantages to a removable compass; it can be used on shore or repositioned to eye level for easier sighting and is available for hiking and other sports. The main disadvantage would be forgetting to take it along.

Another good reason for a mounted compass is that you may not have a free hand to level a hand-held unit while trying to read it. Picture yourself on a bumpy crossing and trying to do this. Having a

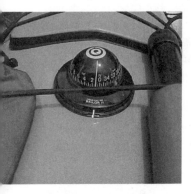

deck-mounted compass allows your bow to become the pointer and makes it much easier to read the direction you're headed. Deck-mounted compasses are self-levelling.

Mounted compasses are most commonly deck- or flush-mounted, though bracket-mounted models are also available. A deck-mounted compass is attached directly to the surface of the kayak, while a flush-mounted model is recessed or built into the deck and is sleeker and lower than a deck-mounted one. As it's already part of your boat, a

A deck-mounted compass is easy to read.

mounted compass is one less thing to worry about when packing and unpacking. A large, mounted compass is easy to read. For serious kayakers, a good recommendation is to have a mounted compass for paddling and a hand-held model for working off charts.

Hand-held compasses range from less than $1 to very expensive. Models good enough for most kayakers' needs range from $15 to $100. A strap-on compass costs around $45 and mounted versions are priced from $45 to about $100, plus installation.

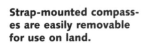

Strap-mounted compasses are easily removable for use on land.

Reading a compass

Compasses come in various styles, shapes and sizes; how you read one will depend on what kind you are using. Most come with instructions. The compass, like all circles, is divided into 360 degrees. Each degree on the compass represents a direction or navigational bearing. North is 0 degrees, east 90 degrees, south 180 degrees and west 270 degrees. A compass is influenced by the earth's magnetic field and is calibrated to point to magnetic north, the earth's magnetic pole. The magnetic pole and the true pole are in different places. The deviation of a compass needle from true north to mag-

Take a moment to check your compass bearings and distances before paddling away.

netic north is known as magnetic declination. Magnetic declination varies with location and changes over time.

Compass rose

A compass rose is a marking on a chart that indicates compass bearings. On marine charts, there are usually two or three compass roses. The roses are usually pink and made up of two graduated circles. The outside circle, which is marked above zero with a star, indicates true north. The inner circle has an arrow pointing to magnetic north. The magnetic declination for a certain year is written along the arrow. For example, on Chart 3311 (Sunshine Coast), the arrow is marked "021°E 1993 (8'W)." Therefore, the magnetic declination was 21 degrees to the east, in 1993. Most compass reading errors involve conversion from true to magnetic north.

How to read a chart with a compass

What's the simplest way to get magnetic bearings from a hydrographic chart? After trying several methods, we have settled on this procedure, which uses only magnetic north:

1. Draw a line on the chart between the points you will be kayaking from and to.
2. Orient your hand-held compass so the north needle points to 0 degrees (north is usually the red portion of the needle).

3. Identify the inner circle of the compass rose (the inner circle has an arrow pointing to magnetic north) on the hydrographic chart.
4. Place the compass on the chart's compass rose.
5. Rotate the chart until the magnetic north arrow on the compass rose lines up with the hand-held compass.
6. Without moving the chart, move the centre of the compass over the drawn line. The magnetic north needle should still be pointed at 0 degrees on the hand-held compass. Read the bearing from the outer ring of the compass using the drawn line as a pointer.
7. Record the bearing on the line (on your hydrographic chart).
8. Once you are under way, follow the bearing from step 7, if using a mounted compass. Hand-held compasses can be used in a similar fashion, if the outer ring is set to 0 degrees. Most hand-helds allow you to swing the outer ring to your bearing and then use the compass's sighting system to find the direction you want to travel. There are a few variations regarding sighting methods but the proper use will be included with the compass's instructions.

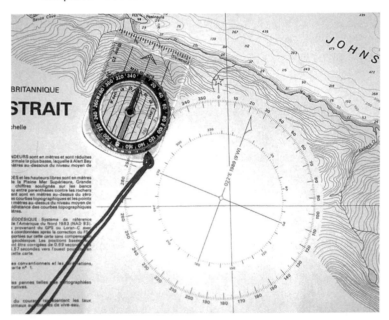

Rotate the chart until the compass rose and compass line up.

We strongly recommend practicing these methods beforehand. You'll become more confident and proficient at plotting a real course and following it by compass.

A hydrographic chart is laid out for true north readings, rather than magnetic readings. Longitude and latitude are based on true north. When you want to quickly grab a bearing off the chart, and can't easily orient it to magnetic north, the longitude and latitude lines enable you to estimate bearings within 10 to 15 degrees. To get a magnetic bearing, you have to remember to subtract the magnetic declination.

Tips for compass and chart use
- A compass, tape measure (for measuring distances on a chart) and a marine chart are part of your essential equipment list.
- Figure out your compass bearings and distances at home, whenever possible.
- On a 1:40,000-scale chart, one inch represents one kilometre of paddling (on a 1:80,000-scale chart, one inch represents two kilometres of paddling).
- Check for nearby metal objects and electrical interference because they can distort compass readings.
- Keep the compass balanced or level when reading it (the needle must be free-floating).
- Establish a land point with your compass, for visual sighting.
- Allow for wind and current drift.

Our experiences (Paul)
"Fogust" (fog in August) is a common weather condition in the Pacific Northwest. Gary and I have had to rely on our compasses or GPS units more than once on a foggy August day while crossing an expanse of water. Fog rolls in quickly and can encompass a large area in a matter of minutes, if not seconds. You don't want to be bobbing, motionless, in the water for too long, listening to the foghorn of some large boat.

More than once, with hat brims pulled low, we've paddled into the blinding sun while using compasses to maintain course. Some days, the islands in the far distance appear as one land mass from our low vantage point and a compass becomes beneficial in guiding us to our destination.

Experience reading a compass and chart really helps if you've made a navigation error. On a recent trip to the Broken Group, the bearing I'd calculated was about 20 degrees off. Somewhere between the Stopper Islands and Lyall Point, a 45-minute crossing, I realized I hadn't subtracted the magnetic declination for the area (20.5 degrees). I'm a trained surveyor, with years of experience, but do make mistakes once in a while and it was fortunate we had more than one person reading a compass that day.

USING A GPS UNIT

A GPS (global positioning system) unit requires signals from three satellites, in order to precisely calculate your location. The word "precise" may be stretching the truth a bit, as using a GPS can be far from that. Years ago, when we first started navigating by GPS, an error was intentionally built into the satellite signals, for military reasons. Even if you programmed your unit properly, accuracy could be off by 100 metres, which is a wide margin of error in fog or darkness. Once that intentional error was removed, using a GPS got a lot better. If used correctly, it's a great navigational tool. Prices start at about $100, but if you want mapping and a built-in compass, expect to pay $300 to $400.

Features
Compass
One of the shortcomings of a GPS is that it isn't a compass. In other words, if you are not moving at a decent speed, it can't tell which way to head to get to where you want to go. Some of the newer models have overcome this by building a compass into the unit.

When used correctly a GPS is a great navigational tool.

Route tracking
Many GPS models have a route-tracking feature that makes it easy to retrace the squiggly line of your route and will even beep if you go off route. This feature is good if you become lost and want to return to your starting point or for forging a new route back to that location.

Mark, waypoint and go-to functions

Almost all GPS units have a mark function. Pushing a button enters your location and you can assign it a name. That location will show on your route, if you have a tracking feature. You can also program in waypoints, which is similar to using a mark except that you don't have to be at the location. To enter a waypoint, you need to accurately enter its longitude and latitude. If you have a go-to function, you can pick a waypoint and tell the GPS to guide you to it. The GPS will give the bearing and point you in the right direction, as long as you are moving and it can find three satellites. Many models will tell you how far you have to go to a waypoint and how soon you will get there, if you maintain your current bearing and speed. As kayakers often follow coastlines and travel around islands, these distance and time estimations aren't usually very accurate.

Speed and distance

Most models will clock your speed and the distance you have covered. You can program for knots, km/h or mph. Although using these features is fun and interesting, they won't often help you find where you want to go.

Other features

You might want some of these other features:
- built-in or computer entering of maps
- battery time-left indicator
- satellite mapping and strength indication
- display of longitude and latitude (very important for a mayday call)
- light for night use

There are many additional features available, such as moon and sun information and fishing bite times.

Tips for using

Your GPS will come with a user's manual that may have been translated into English. The manuals aren't known for ease of use. Community education workshops and paddling club workshops are available in many areas to help people learn to use a GPS. There are instructional videos and books written on the subject.

One of the most important aspects is the accurate entering of waypoints (your destinations). Each degree of longitude and latitude contains 60 minutes and, traditionally, parts of minutes are expressed in seconds. They can also be expressed in a decimal format, however, and this can cause confusion. For instance, 1 minute 15 seconds of latitude is the same as 1.25 minutes. Fortunately, GPS units can be set up in either format.

One minute of latitude equals one nautical mile (1.85 km), so a small error or sloppy measuring can result in your GPS telling you to go right when you should go straight. For many areas, books of GPS waypoints are available. For kayaking, though, your best bet is to use a chart and calipers, or a ruler, to read the coordinates for your waypoints.

Most GPS units are slow to program unless they can be connected to a computer. For an average four-day trip, it usually takes us about two hours to read coordinates and hand-program them.

Mountains can block signals and your GPS will be useless unless you can acquire at least three satellites. This can become a problem even far offshore. The elevation feature on some GPS models can be turned off to set the unit to two dimensions (for use on water). This will normally give better accuracy.

TIDES AND CURRENTS

Tides

Tide predictions for British Columbia and Puget Sound are available in the *Tide and Current Tables, Volumes 5, 6* and *7*, published yearly by the Canadian Hydrographic Service. An hour needs to be added from April to October for Pacific Daylight Time. Knowing the tides ahead of time or having a tide booklet along for reference during your paddle can help you make prudent plans and decisions along the way. Tide times may vary slightly depending on the distance from the table reference point of the area you are paddling. Here are a few tide-related suggestions:

- Knowing the tidal flow will help you predict currents so you can paddle with, instead of against, them.
- Knowing when slack tide or minor tide changes occur will make it safer to travel through narrows or passages with strong currents.
- Knowing how high the tide will come up overnight while camping on a beach can be important when choosing a tent site.

Navigation

Travelling with the wind and currents makes for an enjoyable paddle.

- Launching and landing boats during a medium or high tide is often preferable (shorter carrying distances).
- Travelling up the mouth of a river can often be accomplished during a high tide.
- Exploring inlets, lagoons, small passages and between islands may be more feasible during a slack or higher tide.
- Tying your boat up because the tide will soon be higher is a good idea (we've heard at least one story of a kayak floating away in the night).
- Beaches are bigger and beachcombing is better at low tides.

There are local advertisers who produce free tide-table booklets. The free ones often predict tides in feet and not in metres but that's not an issue for most people. The free ones are also usually corrected for daylight savings time. Because they are small, we always keep one in a zip-lock bag in the back pocket of our PFDs.

The Internet is also a great way of getting tide information for any location on the coast. The Canadian Hydrographic Service site (www.lau.chs-shc.dfo-mpo.gc.ca) is a good resource for paddlers because you can print out tide tables for specific areas and dates. The

Reference page at www.easykayaker.com has tide links for Canada and the US and also lists tidal reference points to use for looking up tides for each area. Some sites give only short-term predictions while others give the longer term.

Currents

A normal cruising speed for a kayak is around 4 knots (7 km/h). Several of the Gulf Islands passes can flow at more than 5 knots (9 km/h), making them impossible to paddle against and very danger-ous to paddle with. (Dodd Narrows can flow at close to 10 knots or 18 km/h.) No one wants to experience being sucked into a 10-m (33-ft) whirlpool in a kayak. You should, consequently, enter a nar-rows during or near slack water, which is usually when the tide is changing direction. A small window of time is normally open to make it through the pass although larger boats will also choose this time.

The *Tide and Current Tables* provide slack-water and maximum-flow times in relation to reference stations and secondary stations. The secondary stations have adjusted times and current speeds that apply to more specific areas. You can locate the more dangerous passes by referring to these tables and also by looking for current arrows on the marine charts. On the charts, a letter A in a diamond gives the location of a current station. Beginning kayakers often miss this symbol and enter into dangerous water conditions unwittingly.

The waters beyond some of the fast-moving passes can also be affected for quite a distance. You may be drawn into a pass or encounter a tidal rip if you are too close to the mouth. A tidal rip is a sideways flow of water caused when two currents moving in dif-ferent directions meet. Normally, the rip occurs where the streams converge at an islet, rock or point, which may cause them to ricochet off in a new direction.

With four tides occurring over an approximate 25-hour period, it's likely you will experience a flood, ebb or both during your paddle. A combination of a 1- to 3-knot (2- to 6-km/h) current and a head-wind can turn the joy of gliding easily through the water into work. On one of our trips, we paddled northeast across Maple Bay with its light rippling waves, past Arbutus Point and into Sansum Narrows, where we suddenly met adverse conditions. A tidal rip, higher winds and a disturbed sea fed by rebounding waves rocked our boats in a variety of directions. Other trips through False Narrows and Gabriola

Navigation

Passage gave us little trouble with wind but the currents contained back eddies that often made steering interesting.

Although currents are directly related to tides, their timing and strength are not necessarily directly related. Slack tide and slack water can differ by over three hours and often differ by 30 to 60 minutes. One of the best ways to know what the current will be doing is to use the *Current Atlas—Juan de Fuca to Strait of Georgia*, published by the Canadian Hydrographic Service. It costs about $25 and consists of 94 charts showing current flows for the area from Campbell River to Port Angeles.

The *Current Atlas* can be used year after year, if you also have a set of *Murray's Tables* for the current year. *Murray's Tables* cost about $8 and are available from Crown Publications (www.crownpub.bc.ca) and from many marine supply stores. By looking up each hour you will be paddling, you can predict currents for your entire route.

So close you can taste the spray of the waterfall.

CHARTS

Maps are no substitute for charts. Many kayak and marine shops carry free copies of the *Pacific Coast Catalogue: Nautical Charts and Related Publications*, issued by the Canadian Hydrographic Service and by the NOAA's Office of Coast Safety. You can use this catalogue to locate and purchase charts specific to the areas you will be paddling. Charts are best kept in large zip-lock bags or soft-plastic marine chart cases. A laminated chart can be tucked under the shock cords just forward of your cockpit. Most kayakers prefer using the chart cases instead of buying laminated charts, which are harder to fold. Sealine manufactures several sizes of chart cases. These are made for all kinds of boating and some can be rather large for kayaking. The 30 by 41-cm (12 by 16-in) size fits well under the bungees on the front deck of most kayaks.

Most marine charts for BC and Puget Sound waters are at a scale of 1:40,000, although some are at 1:20,000 and some at 1:80,000. The 1:40,000 scale is ideal for kayaking. One inch equals one kilometre on the charts at this scale. As we normally travel at 3 to 4 knots (6 to 7 km/h), it's easy to predict paddling and crossing times if winds and currents don't play too large a factor. Usually a chart of this scale can be folded to fit the chart case so that one day's paddle can be covered without having to refold.

Charts contain useful information about tidal flows, which are represented by arrows or the symbol A inside a diamond. The feathered arrow represents current for a flood tide; the unfeathered arrow represents an ebb tide. Fisheries and Oceans Canada also publishes a booklet called *Symbols, Abbreviations and Terms*, which sells for about $6. This booklet helps you interpret all the symbols and notes on marine charts, including geological features.

If you plan on travelling long distances, through groups of islands or in the fog, knowing how to use a marine chart is wise. Even when each paddler has a chart, we don't always agree on where we are. At these times, we are usually rafted together in our kayaks and floating in some cove, but where is that cove, exactly? Yes, such moments do occur.

Navigation

9 Etiquette and wildlife

KAYAKER ETIQUETTE

A friend once said, "If you're not polluting and making noise, you're not having fun." He was joking, but for some boaters, that's not far from the truth. Fortunately, most kayakers are a different breed. On the whole, we are caring people who enjoy nature and respect the environment.

If you were a sea kayaker 10 years ago, you were most likely also a serious outdoors person with a lot of wilderness savvy. The number of people kayaking is growing by about 20 percent a year in British Columbia. Many new kayakers are also new to wilderness camping. The number of kayak campers has grown much faster than the number of campsites and our impact is no longer minimal.

Conflicts are becoming more frequent between kayakers and landowners, First Nations, power boaters and other kayakers. Most of these conflicts stem from a lack of awareness. Unfortunately, as a

Enjoy wildlife from a distance.

result of these conflicts, private lands traditionally used by kayakers are now being closed to camping and the overall reputation of kayakers has suffered. With this in mind, we offer the following etiquette guidelines:

Etiquette for launching and paddling

- Many kayakers use boat ramps as launch sites. Many boat ramps were built with funds and labour donated by power boaters. Be sensitive to the needs of power boaters when sharing a ramp.
- Respect private property rights above high tide, and shellfish lease areas below high tide.
- Respect cultural sites and leave artifacts alone.
- If you are paddling with people less experienced, assume the role of leader and look out for your group's safety and comfort. Lend a hand to help other kayakers launch and land.
- The kayak in front of you has the right of way. Rudders are easily damaged if struck by a following kayak. Don't bump into the kayak ahead.
- Do not step over another person's kayak.
- Do not move someone's kayak without asking. This rule can be broken if the tide is about to float it away or danger is imminent.
- Use your whistle sparingly and for safety purposes only. Have

First Nations heritage sites dot the Pacific Northwest.

Etiquette

a group code: one long blast means all stop and help, two short blasts means all stop and wait.

- Practise low-impact environmental paddling and leave nothing behind, not even fruit peels.
- Consider how your travel will affect marine wildlife. Your paddling should not alter the behaviour of wild creatures. It's okay to observe but give marine mammals a wide berth. If you scare sea birds off their nests by landing on or passing near an island, the eggs or young can quickly be gobbled up by the competition (see Wildlife viewing guidelines, page 149).

Etiquette for camping

- Camp in designated campsites wherever possible. This confines the impact to specific areas.
- Camping below the high-tide line is an option, if the tides cooperate.
- Try to camp away from water sources and trails, to avoid having an impact on wildlife.
- Minimize the urge to tame the jungle. Campsites should be found, not made. BC's unique flora and fauna can be very fragile.
- Stick to existing trails and pitch your tent in established areas.
- Use fire sparingly or, better yet, not at all. In most areas, there are no quick ways to put out a fire that gets out of control. Even if your fire is well confined, the potential risk that it causes may be enough to upset other people visiting the area.
- Leave no trace that you have been there, especially when camping outside designated campsites. Pack everything out, including peelings and food scraps. If you packed it in, pack it out. But why stop there? Why not take away litter left by someone else to help make up for your impact? Leaving an area cleaner than you found it can give you a real sense of pride.
- Here comes the touchy part: human waste and toilet paper. Too many kayakers are leaving these for others to find. Besides being unsightly and unhealthy, human waste also attracts animals. The easiest solution is to camp where an outhouse is available. Other alternatives include using a honey bucket or, as a last resort, digging and using a cat hole. Cat holes should be at least 100 m (325 ft) away from fresh-water

sources and shellfish leases, and not near camping areas or beaches used for swimming.

- Low-impact dishwashing means disposing of grey water far from fresh-water sources and intertidal life. Use no soap or small amounts of eco-friendly soap. If possible, use sand for dishwashing, as even biodegradable soap will affect intertidal life forms.

- As kayak camping grows in popularity, you may find yourself sharing your campsite with others. Even if you were there first, the campsite is not really "yours." Some people are night owls and others are early risers. Campers should minimize noise between 10 p.m. and 8 a.m. Loud radios and pets should be left at home.

A few people camping on a beach each year have little impact. Hundreds, and even thousands, now camp at many of the best kayaking spots in the Pacific Northwest and the impact is becoming significant. Sea kayaking is a fantastic sport and 99 percent of those who take it up are wonderful, caring folk. This chapter is not intended to criticize anyone, only to help reinforce common-sense behaviours and attitudes.

Kayak Routes of the Pacific Northwest Coast, edited by Peter McGee, is an excellent source for more extensive information on minimal-impact camping.

Low-impact camping means leaving nothing behind.

WILDLIFE VIEWING GUIDELINES

Viewing wildlife is an enriching experience. When the paddler actually views marine creatures from a distance, rather than interacting with them, the animals can continue to live comfortably in their home environment. When wild animals are unduly disturbed and their health and welfare are affected, this is harassment. We must try to minimize our impact.

The Pacific Northwest is home to a diverse and complex marine life. While one kayaker, or a group of kayakers, may leave only a soft footprint on the environment, we must all try to reduce the pressures that already exist on stressed animal populations and ecosystems. By paddling too close to animals that are breeding or raising their young, we may disturb them and threaten their survival. The following guidelines are intended to help you enjoy a wildlife encounter and minimize the risk of harassment.

Eagles will be watching!

Marine birds

In the Pacific marine ecozone, we are fortunate to have numerous marine bird species, including puffins, murrelets, ducks, geese, eagles, osprey, oystercatchers, petrels, murres, auklets, guillemots and cormorants.

- Stay at least 100 m (325 ft) from bird colonies and nesting birds.
- Marine birds nest on islets, cliffs and shorelines. Their nests are usually hidden or camouflaged. Check your chart for sensitive areas and use common sense when near nesting sites.
- Sea caves should not be entered during the nesting season.
- Predatory birds will take advantage of parental absence to raid nests; watch for parental behaviour such as a "broken-wing" distraction display to alert you to a nearby nest.

- Estuaries are important feeding and resting areas for young birds and migrating flocks.
- Respect ecological reserves identified on marine charts.

"There are only 11,000 oystercatchers left in the world. Between April and August, they build camouflaged nests near the shoreline of small islets or spits. These are easy to disturb without even knowing you've done so."
—Georgia Strait Alliance (www.georgiastrait.org)

Marine mammals

Marine mammals have behaviours that are peculiar to their families or species. For example, harbour seals rest on haulouts for several hours a day to sleep, socialize and regulate body temperature. Remember that marine mammals may not only be disturbed by your kayak but also by many other kayakers and boaters. A little understanding of animal behaviour can help lighten our impact.

Seals and sea lions
- Stay at least 100 m (325 ft) from all marine mammals.
- Stay at least 200 m (650 ft) from a seal or sea-lion haulout. These sites may include beaches, rocks, floats or even log booms; rookeries normally require a greater buffer zone. Consult Fisheries and Oceans Canada (1-800-465-4336) or the National Ocean Service (301-713-3060) for more information.
- Back off if seals or sea lions move toward the water or show other signs of being disturbed.
- Pups and their mothers are especially vulnerable during nursing time.
- Observe inquisitive seals or sea lions from your kayak at whatever distance the animal chooses; depart on a course away from the animal.

Sea otters
At one point, hunters and traders had completely eliminated the sea otter from our waters. After a successful reintroduction, sea otters have made a comeback. Their behaviour is different from that of seals or sea lions. Their amazingly dense fur and high metabolism requires that considerable time be spent on grooming, resting and

Etiquette

hunting for food. By disturbing any of these activities, kayakers can cause stress to the animals.

- Approach sea-otter habitat with caution and avoid disturbing the animals.
- Observe from at least 100 m (325 ft). Use binoculars for better viewing.
- Sit quietly while observing and start off slowly when leaving.
- Stay well away from crying pups and mothers with pups. Pups are left alone when mothers hunt. Your presence may inhibit and delay the mother from returning to her pup.

Whales, dolphins and porpoises

Whales occasionally surface close to kayaks in areas such as Clayoquot Sound and Johnstone Strait. These animals must be respected for their size and special needs.

- Observe from at least 100 m (325 ft). Use binoculars for better viewing.
- Alert feeding whales to your presence by slapping the water around your kayak or drumming lightly on your deck.
- Kayak parallel to travelling whales and do not position yourself directly ahead of them.
- Limit the time spent observing whales to 30 minutes.
- The *Canadian Fisheries Act* (section 78) allows for fines of up to $500,000 and prison terms up to two years for disturbing or harassing whales.

Binoculars are a great for watching marine mammals.

Intertidal zone

- Small animals that hide in the intertidal zone are susceptible to pollutants such as soap.
- Replace overturned rocks in their original positions when exploring intertidal zones.

SAFETY GUIDE TO BEARS, COUGARS AND WOLVES

Documented attacks on humans by bears, cougars and wolves average only about one per year for all of BC. You are more likely to have a car accident on your way to your launch site than to be involved in an animal attack. Animal encounters, on the other hand, happen frequently.

A cougar recently attacked a young girl on an island not far from Alert Bay. She was sitting with her kayaking group when the animal came out of the bush and attacked her, probably because she was a child. Fortunately, group members were close at hand and drove the cat off.

On Garden Point near Nuchatlitz on Vancouver Island, a kayak was torn to pieces by a bear because a fish had been stored in it. There is no record, though, of anyone being killed by a bear on Vancouver Island.

The same is true for wolves. In BC, wolf attacks on humans are rare. In 2000, a kayaker who was sleeping on Vargas Island was injured by a wolf. The animal had been fed by other kayakers and had been eating human waste, causing it to lose its fear of mankind. This attack prompted BC Parks to install outhouses in the area and to destroy two wolves.

Most wild animals are afraid of people and avoid them. Even so, there is a real possibility of encountering a bear, cougar or wolf in much of the Pacific Northwest. Even Vancouver and Victoria have occasional bear and cougar sightings. Victoria's Empress Hotel has had a cougar wander into its underground parking garage. Fortunately, the cat was tranquilized and relocated. Each year, however, due mostly to human carelessness, too many wild creatures have to be destroyed.

Reading signs and recognizing habitat

Look for the following indicators of active animals in your area:

- Footprints: wolf prints have toenail marks, cougar prints don't.
- Spore: scat colour, smell and moistness will reveal how fresh it is. What's in the spore says a lot, also. If garbage or plastic is found in scat, you likely have a more dangerous, habituated animal.
- Trails: that great hiking trail you're walking on may also be used by animals.
- Scratch trees: cougar scratches are very deep and narrow, and cougars tend to scratch small-diameter trees. Bear scratch marks are less sharp and much more powerfully made.
- Digging: this is usually done by a bear. If someone has buried garbage, however, it could be a bear, cougar or wolf.

Limiting your interactions with wildlife

- Do not approach wildlife.
- Hang food from trees and well away from your tent. Keep food in airtight containers to avoid odours. Use bear caches, if available.
- Fish smells attract bears, cougars and wolves. Clean fish and dispose of bones and leftovers in the ocean, well away from camp.
- Do your cooking, eating and dishwashing well away from your tent.
- Do not leave garbage nearby. Burning tin cans and foil doesn't erase all odours from them.
- Do not bury garbage. Store it safely and then pack it out.
- Do not bring food, toothpaste, gum, insect repellent, deodorant or perfume into your tent.
- Do not store food or garbage in your kayak and never put fresh fish in a storage hatch, even for a few minutes (the smell will linger).
- Never feed wildlife. Animals can become aggressive or dependent. Should an animal become habituated, it will eventually have to be killed ("a fed bear is a dead bear," as the saying goes).
- Do not camp along wildlife trails or near fresh-water sources.
- Avoid going near dead animals. They may be aggressively defended.
- Always keep children nearby and in sight.
- Hike trails and make portages as a group.

- Make noise while walking in the woods by talking, clapping or whistling. Some people wear bells. In other words, try not to surprise a bear, cougar or wolf and put it into a defensive position.
- Leave pets at home or keep them on leashes. A dog can agitate a bear and lead it back to you. A dog may be seen as prey by a cougar and attacked while you are walking it, even if it's on a leash.

If you encounter wildlife

- Stay calm.
- Talk to the animal in a confident voice.
- Pick up small children.
- Face the animal and back off slowly. DO NOT TURN AND RUN.
- Leave the animal an escape route.
- Try to look large (a great excuse for not dieting).
- Don't look the animal in the eye.
- Don't smile or show your teeth.
- Dropping an object such as your daypack may distract the animal and give you extra time to get away.
- If a bear is standing up, it's trying to identify you.
- Bears, cougars and wolves may show signs that they are disturbed and about to become aggressive. These include flattening the ears, raising the hair on backs and necks, showing or snapping the teeth, lowering the head and tasting the air with the tongue.
- Bears make woofing sounds when upset.
- Cougars and wolves growl when upset and becoming aggressive.
- Report any encounters with habituated animals to park staff or wildlife officials.

Attacks

Animals will often defend a personal space that may extend from a few metres to a few hundred metres. If you have put a bear in a defensive position and it attacks from surprise, try to retreat but don't turn and run. A bear will sometimes charge and turn away at the last moment, as a form of bluffing. Your response to a defensive attack should be not to threaten the animal further.

Etiquette

A neighbour was mountain biking once with a few friends on a narrow trail. The lead biker rounded a curve and discovered a bear cub running in front of him. "Where's mom?" he immediately thought. He looked back to find her hot on his trail, swiping at his rear tire. He accelerated and kept looking back until he crashed. The mother bear was caught between him and the other bikers. The fellow on the ground pulled his bike over himself to give the bear room to get by. It worked and no one got hurt.

If a bear attacks offensively (stalks you or attacks you in your tent), fight back. Shout and act aggressively. Do not play dead. Use sticks, rocks or whatever is at hand. Grizzly bears are the only exception to this rule. Grizzly habitat is normally restricted to the BC mainland and islands north of Bute Inlet. Things can change, however; in 2003, the first confirmed grizzly was seen and shot on Vancouver Island, near Port Hardy.

A bear will usually show warning signs before attacking. It will flatten its ears back and raise the hair on the back of its neck. At this point, the hair on the back of your neck should also be reacting. Cougars and wolves are not often seen but may be watching you only a short distance away. Children are the most at risk from attack.

Protection

Your first line of defence against bears is usually to make noise by banging pots and shouting, and to wave sticks. But what happens when a bear wanders into camp and refuses to leave or tries to rip open a kayak?

Pepper spray is the main deterrent carried to repel attacks. Spray containers are small and lightweight, which makes them easy to carry. Spray is not foolproof or 100 percent effective, though. It has a short shelf life before losing potency and needs to be replaced on a regular basis.

Guns are dangerous, heavy and large. Permits are required to purchase and carry firearms. A 12-gauge stainless-steel shotgun with a short pistol grip is best suited for defence in the bush. Most experts suggest loading it with #2 shot, although some suggest alternating 00 shells with slugs. An aggressive animal should have a round fired into the dirt in front of it. This will send small bits of debris flying its way. A word of caution, though: guns can be more dangerous than wild animals.

Bear bombs are another deterrent. These noisemakers are

designed to scare off animals. Occasionally, someone will aim a bear bomb poorly and it will land and explode behind the animal. The startled creature may proceed to run right at the person who fired the bomb, which is not at all what the shooter had intended.

Bears

Bears can travel a long way in a 24-hour period, and in most cases, are just passing through unless attracted by food or garbage. Most bears will resist temptation; those that can't, become known as "food-conditioned" or "habituated." When this happens, they lose their natural fear of humans. They are, after all, bigger and stronger than we are.

Because bears are unpredictable, they can be very dangerous. Bears can run as fast as horses, uphill or downhill, for short distances. They are fine swimmers. Black bears are good tree climbers. That doesn't leave many options for getting away from one.

Black bears average about 90 cm (3 ft) in height at the shoulder and can weigh from 57 to more than 270 kg (125 to 600 lb). They tend to frequent forested areas with low-growing plants and areas with berry bushes. When salmon are spawning, you can find them in salmon-bearing streams and creeks. Bears have excellent hearing and sense of smell. They see fairly well and are strong enough to tear a car apart.

The most dangerous bears are those habituated to human food, defending fresh kills, agitated by dogs or human disturbance (such as pounding on the side of the dumpster when the bear is in it), and females defending cubs.

Cougars

In the past 100 years, five people are known to have been killed in BC by cougar attacks. Four of these were on Vancouver Island. During the last 100 years, there have been 30 non-fatal attacks. While the chance of an attack may be small, a cougar's presence is not to be taken lightly. This animal is capable of killing a 270-kg (600-lb) moose.

Also known as mountain lions and panthers, cougars are BC's largest cat. Adults weigh between 40 and 90 kg (90 and 200 lb). The tail is about one-third the length of the body. A cougar's main prey is deer but it will kill and eat most smaller animals and birds. Although most active at dusk and dawn, a cougar will hunt at all hours of the day and night.

At age two, young cougars go off on their own. They often travel a long distance, looking for an unoccupied territory. This is when they are most likely to get into trouble with humans.

Cougars have retractable claws that distinguish their prints from wolf and dog prints. They are solitary creatures. If you see more than one set of tracks, chances are it's a mother with kittens.

Cougars have little fear and they are attracted by small pets and children. Children make high-pitched sounds and erratic movements and can become scared easily. These qualities may confuse a cat into thinking the child is prey.

Carry a stout walking stick when hiking in cougar country and watch for signs. If you discover a fresh kill, leave the area. Cougars often cover the unconsumed portions of a kill with leaves and soil.

Wolves

Wolves are pretty much large wild dogs and should be treated as such. They have many admirable traits but are also camp robbers and eaters of garbage and human excrement. Because of the sloppy habits of some campers, wolves can easily become habituated and lose their fear of humans.

Wolves have been known to mate with dogs, resulting in hybrid offspring that exhibit both the aggressiveness of a wolf and the domestic qualities of a dog. These animals are often habituated to humans.

If you encounter a wolf, act as a group to instill fear in it. Shout, wave arms and sticks, or throw rocks or sand.

For more information about bear, cougar and wolf safety, visit the websites of BC Parks and BC Environment at:
wlapwww.gov.bc.ca/wld/pub/bearwld.htm
wlapwww.gov.bc.ca/bcparks/explore/safety/visit_safe.htm
The Washington Department of Fish and Wildlife provides information at wdfw.wa.gov.

Our experiences (Gary)

I once had a habituated bear on one side of my tent being agitated by a barking dog on the other side. We were camped at Zeballos and I'd been told that two problem bears had been destroyed in the area the week before.

The previous night, in this same campground, there were no bears and no signs of bears. Then more campers arrived and set up a tent on the far side of the site. They told me their dog would soon let us know if a bear was around. I decided to leave the short-barrelled shotgun behind the seat in Paul's truck instead of taking it into the tent, my usual practice.

About 3:30 a.m., the dog started barking furiously next to my tent. I could hear a bear in the dumpster, knocking bottles over and making a lot of noise. Garbage bears are the worst kind, as they are not afraid of human scent. This one wasn't much bothered by barking dogs either.

Paul was still sound asleep in his tent. My tent hasn't had food in it, not even toothpaste, so I felt fairly bear-safe. I wasn't sure about Paul's tent but knew the bear could easily rip out the plastic windows in his truck canopy, where our food was.

I got up, put on my shoes, turned on my head lamp and flashlight, and got the truck keys and the trigger-lock key for the shotgun. When I unlocked the truck and swung the seat forward, the headrest hit the horn, which gave a short toot and woke Paul. I grabbed the shotgun, went back in my tent, removed the trigger lock and fed a few shells into the gun, keeping the firing chamber empty. My plan was to fire a shot in the air, if the bear tried to get into our food.

The bear left about 4:30 a.m. and I tracked its journey through town by the sounds of dogs barking. I got back to sleep soon afterward, and in the morning, discovered a track where the bear had accelerated away from the back of the truck. The distance from the thumb claw to the far claw was 14 cm (5.5 in), so it was a small bear (but big enough to outwrestle me).

We found out, next morning, that someone from town had put two garbage bags containing crab parts into the dumpster. The door on the dumpster didn't have a latch.

One evening, in northern BC, a group of us found ourselves the only people on a remote island. We walked along, as darkness closed in and the moon came out. Not far away, a wolf howled. The group instinctively tightened up—all except our daughter, Katherine, who was six. She howled back. For about 20 minutes, the two of them howled back and forth. It was a memorable experience and may explain the wolf posters, pictures and T-shirts she still collects. A couple of years later, my family and I spent a week at the mouth of the Skeena River. Although we never saw wild animals, there were fresh

Etiquette

wolf prints crossing our paths daily. Bear signs were also plentiful and fresh, so fresh that the scat smelled like newly mowed grass.

I've seen only four cougars in the wild. One dark night when staying alone in a friend's small trailer deep in the woods near Enderby, I stepped outside for a stroll and had a close encounter with a pair of mating cougars. Those were sounds I'll never forget. The power of their screams was awesome. Talk about noisy sex. Needless to say, I cut my stroll short. The next morning, I inspected the area and found a large patch of torn-up ground.

My longest cougar encounter involved an animal in Port Hardy that, sadly, had become used to eating fish guts left at the boat ramp by sport fishermen. This cougar was in no hurry to hide. Early the next morning, it tried to eat a yappy poodle from our campsite. I applauded its choice but the cougar eventually had to be destroyed.

Seeing or hearing a cougar can be a memorable experience. They see us more often than we see them. Let's hope it stays that way.

Happy paddling!

We hope you find *Easykayaking Basics: A Paddling Handbook for the Pacific Northwest* helpful in your own paddling experiences.

Like most activities, kayaking has a learning curve that never ends. Whether you are a beginner or a seasoned paddler, we hope this book will make that curve a bit easier for you. We probably haven't succeeded in answering all your questions, and we may have even raised new ones, but we tried to focus on concerns that continue to surface at the workshops we give and in the emails we receive.

In parting, we would like to say that good equipment and technique are important, but the main things are to stay safe and have fun. We wish you a wonderful time on the water and hope you will enjoy paddling as much as we and so many others do.

Gary Backlund (gary@easykayaker.com)

Paul Grey (paul@easykayaker.com)

Glossary

Abaft/astern – toward a vessel's stern

Adrift – a boat or kayak that is floating loose

Aft – the back of the boat

Assisted rescue – re-entry into a kayak after a wet-exit and performed with another paddler stabilizing the kayak. Does not require the use of a paddle float.

Baidarka – an Aleutian traditional kayak with a forked or bifid bow

Bailer – a can or small bucket used to bail a boat. Most kayaks carry a pump.

Beam – the widest part of a boat. Single kayaks are typically 56 to 61 cm (22 to 24 in) wide.

Bearing – a direction. Kayakers will often establish a reference point (either on a chart or from the water) and follow a compass bearing (angular measurement) from one point to another.

Bent-shaft paddle – a kayak paddle bent for ergonomic reasons. The bends allow wrists to be in a more natural position.

Blade – the wide, flat area of a kayak paddle that grips the water

Bow – the front of the kayak

Brace – pressing the blade of a paddle on the surface of the water to prevent capsizing

Bulkhead – a watertight partition between the cockpit and the storage compartments. Compartments act as positive flotation.

Buoyant heaving line – a 15-m (50-ft) rescue rope that floats and can be thrown

Canadian Collision Regulations – rules for right of way, yielding and travel on water

Canadian Hydrographic Service – government department responsible for producing marine charts, and tide and current tables

Capsize – tipping over

Centre of gravity – the balance point in a kayak. It may be negatively affected if the paddler is sitting too high (on a thick foam pad, for example). This raises the paddler's centre of gravity and affects the tippiness of the kayak. A fully loaded kayak has a lower centre of gravity, making it more stable.

Chart – a map of coastal areas denoting depths, currents, shore and bottom types, plus other aspects of marine and navigational information

Chine – transition from bottom to sides of a boat hull. Soft chine is a rounded hull; hard chine indicates a series of planes.

Coaming – the raised edge around a cockpit. The coaming prevents water from entering and is designed to secure a sprayskirt.

Cockpit – the seating area of a kayak. A closed-cockpit kayak covers most of a paddler's legs. This provides an area for the knees/thighs to brace against, giving the kayaker more control over the boat and allowing better use of the body in paddling.

Compass – device designed to indicate geographic direction

Composite – made up of more than one material. This term is often used to denote fibreglass and Kevlar kayaks.

Day hatch – a small, easily accessible watertight compartment handy for storing small items such as wallet, keys and lunch

Deck – the top surface of a kayak

Declination (or magnetic declination) – the angular deviation measurement (usually in degrees) from true or magnetic north

Draw stroke – a paddle stroke used to move the kayak sideways

Drytop – a watertight paddling jacket

Ebb – a receding tide. The opposite of flood.

Edging – a manoeuvre to turn a kayak tightly by putting it on its edge. This is best performed with reasonable speed and using the paddle to turn the boat.

Eskimo roll – a manoeuvre for self-righting a kayak. It can be used for self-rescue, although sea kayaks are difficult to roll back up for most paddlers.

Feathered paddle – one with paddle blades set to different planes. Many paddles have two or three settings. In stiff winds, a feathered paddle offers an edge, rather than a surface, and reduces resistance.

Flare – the angle of the hull as it grows wider from the waterline to the gunwales. A kayak with a more pronounced flare has greater secondary stability.

Float plan – a description of your launch site, paddling route and estimated time of return. Given to a family member or friend for potential search and rescue purposes.

Flood – an incoming tide

Flotation bag – an inflatable bag used to provide flotation for a swamped boat

Footrests – the foot brace found in the cockpit. Footrests may be called foot pedals. A footrest often is attached to and operates the rudder when lowered.

Gel coat – the hard outer plastic resin surface of most composite kayaks

GPS (Global Positioning System) – an electronic navigation device that uses satellite signals to give location, bearing, distance and speed of travel plus other information

Grab loop – a handle or loop at the front of a sprayskirt, used for quick release during a wet-exit

Glossary

Greenland kayak – a traditional kayak of Greenland with a sleek, raked bow

Greenland paddle – a kayak paddle that has very long, narrow blades that are usually less than 10 cm (4 in) wide

Habituated – a wild animal that has lost its natural fear of man. Usually caused by being food-conditioned.

Hatch – an opening in the kayak's deck, fitted with a cover. Hatch covers may be level with the deck or raised above it and are held watertight by bungee cord or straps or by neoprene covers.

Headwind – a wind blowing against you and slowing your rate of travel

Hold – area for storage in the bow or stern portion of the kayak. Sometimes referred to as a hatch.

Hull – the lower half of a kayak that is in contact with water. Hulls are designed for speed and stability.

Initial stability – how easy it is to rock the kayak in calm conditions. Too much initial stability can affect advanced paddling techniques, such as edging, and decrease a boat's "playfulness." Higher levels of initial stability are better for photography, fishing and daydreaming. See also Secondary stability.

Keel – an extrusion along the bottom of a boat. The keel may not be distinctive on a kayak.

Kevlar – a fabric laminate used in place of fibreglass to reduce weight

Knot – a measure of speed. One knot is one nautical mile per hour. There are approximately 1.85 km (1.15 mi) to a nautical mile.

Land breeze (offshore breeze) – a wind caused by a differential of temperature between land and water bodies that blows out from land and over the water. A land breeze is normally stronger closer to the coastline.

Latitude – lines of latitude run parallel to the equator. The equator is at 0 degrees and the poles are at 90 degrees north and south. One minute of latitude equals one nautical mile.

Lay-up – the way fibreglass or Kevlar is matted to make a kayak or canoe

Lee – the calm area behind an island, peninsula or large object

Lee shore – shore that offers protection from current or wind

Lock-outs – tilting (locked-in-place), foot-controlled rudder pedals

Longitude – lines of longitude run perpendicular to the equator

Mayday – a distress call indicating that someone's life is in immediate danger

Nautical mile – see Knot

Neoprene – a synthetic rubber used for protection against weather and heat loss. Most wetsuits are made of this material.

NOAA's Office of Coast Safety – US government department respon-

for producing marine charts, and tide and current tables

Oil-canning – large dents caused by heat and pressure to rotomoulded kayaks

Outfitter – a person or company that supplies kayaks and paddling equipment. This term is also applied to companies that offer guided kayaking trips.

Paddle – used to propel a kayak through the water. Kayak paddles are constructed from various materials and most have two blades. The paddle may be one-piece, two-piece or four-piece.

Paddle float – a buoyancy device that attaches to the blade of a paddle to assist with a self-rescue (like an outrigger)

Paddle leash – a lightweight, cord-like device for attaching a paddle to the kayak. Used during paddling for both convenience and safety.

Pan-pan – a distress call that someone is in danger. (Mayday is used if there is an immediate threat to life.)

PFD – Personal Flotation Device, typically a Coast Guard Class III buoyant vest. It is a more comfortable jacket than a life vest (or jacket). Kayak PFDs are designed for paddling in comfort.

Pitch – to dip bow and stern alternately

Port – the left side of a vessel. The opposite of starboard.

Primary stability – see Initial stability

PSP – Paralytic Shellfish Poisoning; algae blooms (often known as red tides) can carry minute amounts of toxins, which temporarily build up in bivalves (clams, oysters, mussels) and can be deadly to humans.

Reference and secondary stations – locations where tides or currents are predicted by Canadian Hydrographic Service tide and current tables

Rocker – the curve on the bottom of a kayak or boat along the centre line from bow to stern. A kayak will turn more easily with more rocker. Touring kayaks are designed with less rocker because they are used to travel long, straight distances.

Rotomoulding – a manufacturing process that produces a plastic kayak from a mould. Rotomoulded kayaks can be made much more quickly than fibreglass ones, thus reducing the cost.

Rudder – a device on or near the stern of the kayak for steering. It is raised and lowered by cords and usually operated by footrests or pedals.

Secondary stability – the resistance of a kayak to capsizing. See also Initial stability.

Self-rescue – unassisted re-entry into a kayak after a wet-exit. Best performed with a paddle float and paddle.

Sheer line – the edge where the deck and hull meet. Also known as gunwale.

Shock cords (bungee cords) – elastic cords, often fitted to decks to attach equipment

Skeg – a fin located on the keel near the stern to improve tracking. May be fixed or retractable.

Slack current – occurs when currents are about to change direction due to tidal flow. Does not necessarily occur at the same time as a slack tide and may vary by more than three hours from low or high tide.

Slack tide – occurs at low and high tides and when there is no tidal change for a period of time. Most Pacific Northwest tidal areas have three or four slack tides every 25 hours.

Sliders – sliding, foot-controlled rudder pedals

Small-craft warning – issued when winds are predicted to be 20 to 33 knots (37 to 61 km/h) or higher.

Splash jacket – a lightweight paddling jacket with tight-fitting neck and sleeve cuffs

Sprayskirt – a tight-fitting cover made either from neoprene or nylon (or both) that fits around the kayaker's waist and then around the coaming of a cockpit to prevent water from spilling into the cockpit

Starboard – the right side of a vessel. The opposite of port.

Stern – the rear or aft of a boat

Swell – a long wave that travels a great distance. Height is measured from level ocean (not trough) to wave crest (top).

Tidal rip – a sideways flow of water caused when two streams of water moving in different directions meet

Tide – the diurnal rise and fall of the oceans

Tracking – the tendency of a kayak to travel in a straight line. Longer boats and ones with less rocker tend to track straighter and are harder to turn.

Tunnel – the waist section of a sprayskirt or paddling jacket

UV protectant – a coating on a kayak to retard ultraviolet degradation from the sun

Vacuum bag technology – a method using vacuum pressure to spread resin through laminate when manufacturing kayaks

VHF radio – a two-way radio used for marine communication

Weathercock – the tendency of a boat to turn into the wind. The rudder on a kayak will help control this action.

Wet-entry – re-entering a kayak from the water. See also Self-rescue.

Wet-exit – exiting an overturned kayak. See also Self-rescue.

Wind wave (chop) – a short wave caused by local winds

Yaw – wave action causing your kayak to turn or swing off course

Index

Additional Reading from Harbour Publishing

Kayaking Vancouver Island: Great Trips from Port Hardy to Victoria
By Gary Backlund and Paul Grey
6" x 9" • 295 pages • 1-55017-318-9 • $24.95
Veteran paddlers Gary Backlund and Paul Grey describe more than 20 kayaking trips ranging from a lazy day excursion in Victoria's historic Gorge waterway to an exciting multi-day voyage around Meares Island in Clayoquot Sound. Includes maps, photographs, information on launch sites, camping places, currents and tides.

The Beachcomber's Guide to Seashore Life in the Pacific Northwest
by J. Duane Sept
5.5" x 8.5" • 240 pages, 500 colour photos • 1-55017-204-2 • $24.95
274 of the most common animals and plants found along the saltwater shores of the Pacific Northwest are described in this book. Illustrating each entry is a colour photo of the species in its natural habitat.

Paddling The Sunshine Coast
by Dorothy and Bodhi Drope
5.5" x 8.5" • 192 pages, 40 photos, illustrations and maps •
1-55017-164-X • $19.95
This book will introduce both new and experienced sea kayakers to the matchless paddling opportunities of the Sunshine Coast, from Howe Sound in the south to Desolation Sound in the north, including Sechelt Inlet, the islands of Georgia Strait and Jervis Inlet.

Pacific Reef and Shore: A Photo Guide to Northwest Marine Life
by Rick M. Harbo
5.5" x 8.5" • 80 pages, 300 colour photos • 1-55017-304-9 • $9.95
A brilliant full-colour field guide to the marine life of coastal British Columbia, Alaska, Washington, Oregon and northern California is perfect for divers, boaters, beachwalkers and snorkellers.

Visions of the Wild: A Voyage by Kayak Around Vancouver Island
by Maria Coffey and Dag Goering
8" x 9.5" • 192 pages, colour photos • 1-155017-264-6 • $36.95
Brimming with breathtaking colour photographs and compelling journal entries from all stages of their three-month kayaking journey, this book is at once an inspiring chronicle of an adventure of a lifetime, and a beautiful book of photographs that rejoices in the untamed spirit of Canada's West Coast.